30 DAYS OF PERSON

Women
TOUCHED BY
Jesus

LEIGHANN MCCOY

The quoted ideas expressed in this book (but not Scripture verses) are not, in all cases, exact quotations, as some have been edited for clarity and brevity. In all cases, the author has attempted to maintain the speaker's original intent. In some cases, quoted material for this book was obtained from secondary sources, primarily print media. While every effort was made to ensure the accuracy of these sources, the accuracy cannot be guaranteed. For additions, deletions, corrections, or clarifications in future editions of this text, please write Leighann McCoy.

Unless otherwise noted all Scripture quotations are taken from: The Holy Bible, New International Version (NIV) Copyright © 1973, 1978, 1984, by International Bible Society. Used by permission of Zondervan Publishing House. All rights reserved.

The New American Standard Bible®, (NASB) Copyright © 1960, 1962, 1963, 1968, 1971, 1972, 1973, 1975, 1977, 1995 by The Lockman Foundation. Used by permission.

Greenwood, Glenn, and Latayne C. Scott. *A Marriage Made in Heaven*. Dallas: Word Publishing, 1990.

Author's Photograph by Sonya Swallows / Just Shoot Me Photography

Cover Design & Page Layout by Bart Dawson

ISBN 978-158334-498-9

Printed in the United States of America

30 Days of Personal Bible Study

Women

Touched by

Jesus

Leighann McCoy

THIS BOOK IS DEDICATED TO:

Mothers, grandmothers, aunts, sisters, daughters and best friends forever. It is dedicated to business executives, missionaries, ministers, doctors, lab technicians, public officials, pet groomers and stay-at-home moms. I dedicate this book to women who've lived on the streets, those who've suffered chronic illness, the ones who've watched loved ones die and those who've divorced their husbands.

This book is dedicated to women who have been and will be touched by Jesus.

This book is also dedicated to my husband Tom, and my children Mikel, Kaleigh and TJ—who've graciously allowed me to share our lives with you.

TABLE OF CONTENTS

Introduction

As you complete the personal studies in this book, you will meet women Jesus came into contact with during His earthly ministry. After taking an in-depth look at their experiences through daily studies, you'll take an imaginary journey in their shoes through fictional stories based on their encounters described in Scripture. This will be fun, thought provoking and, I pray, life-changing for you.

There are six chapters focusing on the encounters that eight women had with Jesus. Each chapter contains five personal studies followed by a fictional story. As a bonus, I've included a seventh chapter on the woman who was perhaps touched most intimately by Jesus during His earthly life—this chapter invites you to come alongside Mary, the mother of Christ.

As you complete these studies, you will realize that God has always had a special place for us in His plan. Long ago He trusted women with the news of Jesus' resurrection. Have you ever wondered why He did that? Women were lesser citizens in that day. When Jesus fed the 5,000, the gospel writers were only counting the men. Women were not considered worthy enough to be registered in the count! But, on that first Easter morning, women were trusted with the good news.

I don't really wonder...after all, women just tell stories better than men! Here's how men might have reported the resurrection: "We went to the tomb. His body was gone. He is risen!"

And here's how the women might have told the same story:

"We got up early. We'd decided to do this because we hadn't had time to properly prepare His body for burial because of the Sabbath laws and all. Mary gathered the frankincense, I took the myrrh. On the way there, we wondered how we'd get the stone moved out of the way. But as soon as we arrived, Joanna (you know Jo, she always has to rush ahead! Why, just the other day, [deep sigh] never mind.) Joanna yelled back to us, 'the stone! It's rolled away!' She waited until we got there to walk on in. I was trembling as we approached the slab where they'd laid his body. He was not there! I mean it, bless His sweet heart. He was gone! His grave clothes were folded neatly at the foot of the slab as if He'd taken His time to tidy up before He left! Mary, Joanna and I fell to our knees. We were frightened and excited all at the same time!

Suddenly two marvelous creatures stood before us. They were *like* men but seemed to glow with light! Their robes were pure white! I've never been able to get anything that clean. (I scrub, rinse, scrub...how do you deal with stain? I'm so sorry; I got off the subject again.) Anyway, these men...these heavenly messengers asked us, 'Why are you looking for the living among the dead? He is not here! He's risen just as He said!'"

You get the idea. God knew our nature; that's why He let women spread the news of Jesus' resurrection. He wanted every detail covered and He wanted the news to travel fast! There's nobody who can do a job like that better than a woman.

God has plans for women—specific, unique, special plans. Through these personal studies you will discover that no matter what you've done in your past, no matter what hinders your present, no matter who you're married to, how busy you are, or how long you've been sick, God has a plan for you. You'll learn from the experiences of the women who were touched by Jesus and come face to face with Him yourself.

My hope is that as you pause by the well, sit quietly in the synagogue, press close in the crowd and travel the dusty road, you will find yourself eventually with Mary at the foot of the cross where you will "taste and see that the Lord He is good!" I pray that as you learn to embrace and be embraced by God's perfect love, you will partner with Him in fulfilling your part of His plan. May God richly bless you as you meet Him in these studies and in your daily life.

Charm is deceitful and beauty is vain,
but a woman who fears the Lord,
she shall be praised.

—

Proverbs 31:30

A VERSE TO MEMORIZE

Above all love each other deeply,
because love covers a multitude of sins.

—

I Peter 4:8

CHAPTER 1
Choosing What Is Better

WOMEN TOUCHED BY JESUS
Martha and Mary
Luke 10:38-42

INTRODUCTION
**"Only a few things are necessary,
really only one!"**

As women we suffer from the "just do it!" syndrome. We think a busy woman is a successful woman. A hectic life is a full and meaningful life. Often times our busy-ness causes us great frustration and stress. We get so caught up in the schedule that we lose sight of the things that really matter. Jesus said something to Martha one day that warrants our close attention this week. He said, "Martha, Martha, you are worried and upset about so many things, but only a few things are necessary, really only one!" (Luke 10:41-42 NIV and NASB)

During your daily time alone with God, you will discover what that one thing is. You will be challenged to allow God to show you what must be rearranged in your heart, your mind and your activity in order to give priority to that one thing!

DAY 1
"THE END OF ALL THINGS IS NEAR. THEREFORE ..."

Read I Peter 4:7-11

Intimacy Described

My husband Tom and I are close. In June 2000, Tom was in a serious car accident. He broke ribs and his sternum, busted his knee and toes, and was transported by ambulance to Vanderbilt Hospital in Nashville, TN.

I was out of town. I'd just completed a two-day trip that originated in Ft. Lauderdale, Florida, and ended in Blowing Rock, North Carolina. After dropping Tom off at the Orlando airport, I picked up my sister and her two girls in Gainesville, Florida, and the seven of us traveled in our mini van to Powder Springs, Georgia, to spend the night with my mother and father on our way to spend a week with another of my sisters (Sharon) in North Carolina. My van was loaded with five children, my sister Mitzi, and me. Needless to say, after two solid days of travel I was exhausted.

> *Above all love each other deeply, because love covers a multitude of sins.*
> I Peter 4:8

When we got to Sharon's cabin in the beautiful Blue Ridge Mountains, she mentioned that Tom had called. I assumed he wanted to make sure we'd arrived safely, so I didn't think twice about getting everyone settled and fed before I called him back.

After dinner, I called him at the number he'd left me. (He was at our brother and sister-in-law's house.) As soon as Tom answered I chattered about our long trip and the fun that was scheduled for our week in the mountains. When I finally stopped babbling, Tom said, "I've got some good news and some bad news; which do you want first?"

He sounded like someone had died, so I tried to prepare myself for what was coming and said, "The bad news, I guess."

"Well, the good news is that I am OK!" (He always does that, asks which I want first then gives me what I didn't ask for!) "The bad news is that I had a wreck today."

Immediately I interrupted, "You were talking on the phone, weren't you?!"

Ignoring me, he continued, "The car is totaled."

My heart skipped a beat, "What do you mean totaled? Was anyone hurt?"

I could still tell by what he wasn't saying that I hadn't heard the really bad news yet.

He continued. "They took me to Vanderbilt."

"What's wrong with you?"

"I broke my sternum, a few ribs...but I'm OK. Sarah's taking care of me."

My sister-in-law is a nurse. I sat stunned, trying to let the reality of his mortality soak in. He repeated, "I'm OK."

And in the second "I'm OK" I could hear him really saying, "Please come home!"

I thought of all the preparation Sharon had made on our behalf, and about how excited my three children were to spend the week with their aunts and cousins. I knew they'd be upset if we cut our visit short. But I also knew Tom needed us. He insisted that we stay, but underneath his assurance that he'd be fine, I knew he wanted me with him. I knew I wanted to be with him.

So, amidst everyone's disappointment (my sisters, nieces and children), I packed us up and started home the next morning. Tom didn't ask us to come home. My sisters didn't want me to go home, and my children were upset with me. But I had to do what my heart demanded and go be with Tom.

It wasn't until I arrived home that I realized how close we'd come to losing him. His injuries were serious and required eight weeks to heal. But more than the physical recovery was the emotional shock of having nearly lost him in a car wreck.

I realized Tom McCoy was so much a part of me that without him I'd be less of who I am. I also learned that my physical presence could bring as much comfort to him as his could to me. I also realized that I can't make everyone happy (my sisters and children) and give Tom rightful priority, too. Sometimes I have to choose between what's good for my marriage and what others want from me. And that is ok.

Tom and I didn't experience this kind of intimacy overnight. Through our years together we've *chosen* to be best friends. We've developed our friendship by talking. We talk all the time. We also do things together. We walk, we water ski, and we travel. We spend time together.

Meet God in His Word

In your copy of God's Word, reread I Peter 4:7-8 and:

- Underline the phrase that tells us what time is near.
- Circle the word that tells us why we need to be clear-minded and self-controlled.
- Put a square around that which we should do "above all."

Fill in the Blanks

The end of all things is _____.

Therefore be clear-minded and self-controlled so that you can _____.

Prayer is your vital link to God. Prayer is how you stay connected to His heart.

Face to Face with Jesus:

God wants to be your best friend!

That is exactly why Peter told us to be clear-minded and self-controlled—so we can pray. Prayer is sitting quietly in the presence of God and allowing His simple awesome presence to bring you comfort and courage. Prayer is also choosing to be best friends with God by talking with Him. You can talk to God at a designated time (sometimes our lives get so busy that Tom and I have to schedule breakfast together to discuss our calendars), and you can talk to Him all the time. (I Thess. 5:16 says, "pray without ceasing.")

Most likely, you will have to disappoint some other people in your life to allow God first priority. My prayer for you is that you grow so intimately close to God that you don't know where He stops and you begin. My prayer is that you will allow Jesus to be real in you!

Think of the person you are closest to on earth. Describe that relationship. How did you get to be so close?

Thank God for your relationship with that person. Talk to God about your relationship with Him. What do you appreciate? What do you long for? Ask God to help you be clear-minded and self-controlled so you can pray.

MY PRAYER FOR TODAY

DAY 2
"DO WHATEVER HE TELLS YOU"

Read John 2:7-11

Weddings Now and Then

Jesus told Martha that she worried about "so many things." In Martha's day she might have worried over the necessary preparations for feeding all those guests! There were dates to be gathered, lambs to roast and goats to milk. The serving dishes needed to be cleaned and the home prepared. Dusting, sweeping, arranging furniture, cooking, designing—all of it at last minute's notice!

Have you ever participated in a large family gathering or social event? If you have, think of the many tasks that go into such an affair:

> *Above all love each other deeply, because love covers a multitude of sins.*
> I Peter 4:8

I'm thinking of my wedding: invitations to order, bridal gown to choose, and bridesmaids' dresses (my mother is an excellent seamstress, and she sewed all of these. Of course, three of my five bridesmaids were sisters!), a registry chosen and submitted (of course this includes every last detail—china patterns, crystal, silver, casual dinnerware, stainless steel, utensils, towels, toiletries, sheets, bedroom colors, any number of household furnishings and this alone sent me into a tither!), florist, caterer (complete with endless menu and flower choices), securing a church, preacher (Tom's father performed our wedding), musicians, wedding directory, program, guest list, honeymoon details...the list of "so many things" is mind boggling! Very subtly the focus is taken from the enormous decision being made by the bride and groom "to love and cherish in sickness and in health till death do us part" and instead placed on a zillion details directly related to one 20-minute ceremony!

Now, don't get me wrong. When my girls get married, there will be no wedding in all of middle Tennessee to compare with the wedding I will help them plan. However, we easily replace matters of the heart with matters of the hands. And if we're not careful, the activities we choose to juggle like flaming batons begin to penetrate our hearts and we look around at other people who don't seem nearly so bothered by the details we're being burnt with (as our flaming batons fall), and we snap, "Here I am doing everything while she just sits there enjoying your company!"

I've used a wedding as an example of how easily we can get surrounded by countless details. Let's visit Jesus as He performed His first miracle at...a wedding!

Imagine the preparation that went into a Jewish wedding in Jesus' day. The betrothal, which was legally binding like a marriage, would last about a year. During this year, the bride would prepare for her marriage. The bride did not know her exact marriage date, but if she were a virgin, she knew she would be married on a Wednesday near the completion of a year's betrothal. (Jewish weddings took place on Wednesdays in case the groom discovered the bride was not a virgin on the wedding night, and he could divorce her on Thursday, the day courts were in session. If the bride was a widow, she would be married on Thursday.) The father of the groom made the final decision as to when the wedding would take place, and sometimes he didn't even let his son know until the last minute. The father determined the date of the wedding according to his own finances and by watching the son's preparation of the bridal chamber. "A family's social standing in the community and their reputation depended on the lavishness of the coming celebrations."

When the bridal chamber and the father's finances were in order, the father would send preliminary invitations. These were more like an urgent summons. As soon as the dinner was actually prepared, the guests would be gathered with the second invitation.

During final days, rumors of arriving shipments of wine, butchered animals or new clothes would trickle to the bride and her hand-picked maidens. Every evening the girls would gather at the bride's home, giggle and speculate as to when the actual celebration would begin. Many Tuesday evenings, the bride would dress in her wedding gown, which was a richly embroidered robe with a lavish belt. She would soak herself in spices such as myrrh, her hair would be braided and she would wear all the jewelry she could find—much of it borrowed.

Finally the night would come when the bridegroom, also dressed lavishly, wore a crown prepared by his mother, and marched through the streets with his friends, musicians, and singers hired for the occasion. They would wake up everyone in their path, and the entire community would rejoice in the long awaited night. Upon reaching the bride's home, the party would get very quiet in hopes of surprising the bride. Then, one person was given the job of shouting loudly to wake the family, provide the bride just enough time to get her veil and honeymoon clothes, embrace her parents, receive their final blessing then cease to be part of that family clan to join the groom's the moment she stepped out the door. As soon as she stepped outside, the raucous celebration would begin again, and with her veil held tightly to completely cover her face, the bride would search for the bridegroom in the crowd.

The late night wedding procession would not take a direct course back to the groom's home; instead they paraded throughout the neighborhoods. Once they arrived at the groom's neighborhood, they entered the bridal canopy. Often, the canopy was located in the marketplace. After leaving the canopy, the groom took his bride to the bridal chamber. (Vows were not exchanged in the Jewish ceremony until after Roman times. The actual marriage was official after sexual intercourse.)

Once alone and in the bridal chamber (carefully prepared by the groom), the groom would remove the bride's veil, see her and speak to her with no barriers. The entire wedding party waited in an outer room for news that the marriage had been consummated. The groom's best friend would wait for the groom's confirmation, and then announce the marriage to the waiting guests and the party began.

The bride and groom stayed in the bridal chamber during most of the celebration, but outside the festivities would continue for up to a week. The friends of the groom were to make sure everyone was having a good time. Servants washed the guests' feet with ceremonial water stored in large water jars. Musicians played songs, there was much dancing, food was plentiful and wine flowed freely. The bride and groom would occasionally join the group and when they did they were treated like royalty and even sat on thrones to observe the festivities.

At the close of the week, the groom's father provided a marriage feast. The bride and groom greeted their guests and shared this feast with them. This meal marked the beginning of their life together.
(This information came from *A Marriage Made in Heaven*, Greenwood and Scott, chapters 8-9.)

After reading of the significance of the wedding celebration and feast, can you imagine what a disaster this would be for the father of the groom to run out of wine? Remember, "A family's social standing in the community and their reputation depended on the lavishness of the coming celebrations."
(p. 64, A Marriage Made in Heaven)

Meet God in His Word

Look again at John 2:8-10. What was the customary way to serve wine at a wedding? Fill in the Blanks:

Everyone brings out the _____ wine _____ and then the

_____ wine after the guests have had too much to drink!

(John 2:10)

Somebody didn't pay close enough attention to the details in this wedding party. But Mary knew Jesus could take care of this crisis. And at her kind request, Jesus took the ceremonial water and turned it into fine wine!

Face to Face with Jesus

There are many truths to be gained from this miracle John records as Jesus' first. But the one I want to explore is this:

When you maintain a dynamic personal relationship with God, and you recognize His infinite unmatched power coupled with His perfect love toward you, you will not worry over the details! Like Mary, you will merely mention the dilemma, and go about your business completely confident that Jesus will take care of the situation.

Reread John 2:3-5.
Did Mary respond to Jesus' question? Why or why not?

Mary was quietly confident the matter was safe in His hands no matter what He decided to do.

Jesus chose to perform this miracle perhaps to teach us that no matter how attentive to details we may be, our best cannot begin to compare to His. He may have performed this miracle to remind us that we needn't worry when we're in "a pinch." He is more than capable of getting us out. He may be reminding us today that He is much more interested in our hearts than He is with our hands.

When's the last time you were bogged down in busy-ness? Are you now? What were/are you involved in? What worries were/are connected with these things? List them vertically:

Would you dare go to that list of worries and offer each one to Jesus today? If so, print next to each worry, "I choose to trust You!"

Read John 2:5. What did Mary tell the servants?
You do the same. Today "do whatever He tells you."

MY PRAYER FOR TODAY

DAY 3
"ABOVE ALL ELSE
LOVE ONE ANOTHER DEEPLY..."

Read I Corinthians 13

They Lived Happily Ever After

When life seems to spin recklessly out of control, we desperately need to prioritize. God's Word tells us what is most important. "Above all else, love one another deeply." If we will focus on the priority of love, oftentimes the other pressures of life will disappear.

The problem with our effort toward love is that we don't really know what love is! Satan has craftily created a deceptive form of love that is self-serving, never satisfied, destructive and counterfeit. Too many times we're caught in its tricky web of disaster.

> *Above all love each other deeply, because love covers a multitude of sins.*
> I Peter 4:8

As little girls, the deception begins with seemingly innocent fairy tales. An older woman (witch, evil stepmother, former beauty queen, etc.) persecutes the beautiful fair maiden, and the lovely (rich and powerful) prince endures great danger, overcomes the odds, and rescues her to live "happily ever after." Only the worst deception of fairy tales is that the end is really the beginning! How do these two people get along when he continues to play games with his shiny-armored buddies and she sits alone each night in an empty castle surrounded by a crocodile-filled moat in a foreign land? Who feeds the royal offspring when he seems to be hungry every two hours between midnight and 6 a.m.? How does the gallant prince feel about her when she turns 50 and those once golden locks are gray, and that perfect wispy figure suffers years of plenty to eat, three princesses, two princes and too little exercise?

Cinderella, your prince is only charming if you *choose* to make up your mind that he will seem so to you! Love is emotional to be sure, but it is also something you choose (with your mind) to do (with your hands) regardless (of your heart). Mind (head) over matter (behavior) can influence emotion (heart).

19

Meet God in His Word

In I Corinthians 13 Paul tells us how to experience and exercise real love. Read verses 1-3 and match the following:

If I speak in tongues of men and angels	But have not love	I am nothing
If I have the gift of prophecy	But have not love	I gain nothing
If I have faith to move mountains	But have not love	I gain nothing
If I give all I possess to the poor	But have not love	Noisy gong/cymbal
If I surrender my body to the flames	But have not love	I am nothing

What does this mean to you?

Love is more important than anything I can do—even with God's power working through me! Read verses 4-6 and print what love is and is not.

Love is/does:

Love is not/does not:

There are four things love always does, what are they? (v. 7)

1. Love always _____

2. Love always _____

3. Love always _____

4. Love always _____

There are three things that will pass away and one thing that will not. (vv. 8-12) Complete the following:

Where there are _____, they will _____.

Where there are _____, they will be _____.

Where there is _____, it will _____

_____.

Love _____ _____!

Print that truth again:

Paul recognized that three things remain until the end of time (v. 13). They are:

1. _____

2. _____

3. _____

Which one lasts beyond then into eternity? _____

Print this week's memory verse:

Face to Face with Jesus
Based on today's study of I Corinthians 13, what is love?

How have you expressed love to others? How has love been expressed to you?

What is love not?

Who do you need to love today? How can you do that?

Is there anything you have done *for* God that replaced love? What?

Ask God to forgive you for letting "so many things" crowd out the greatest thing. Ask Him to love others through you today.

MY PRAYER FOR TODAY

DAY 4
"SHE HAD A SISTER CALLED MARY"

Read Luke 10:38-42

Martha's Home

When Jesus came to Mary's home, Luke tells us *Martha* opened *her* home to Him. Mary was most likely the younger sister. Being younger, she was possibly relegated to lesser responsibilities. The weight of the household management lay squarely on Martha's shoulders.

Perhaps Mary intended to see to the guests' comfort before she dismissed herself to the kitchen to help prepare the banquet. But once she spent a few minutes in the presence of Jesus, she was captivated by His love and completely forgot all else that was "demanding" her attention.

> *Above all love each other deeply, because love covers a multitude of sins.*
> I Peter 4:8

How refreshing! A woman absorbed in the presence of Jesus!

Meet God in His Word

In the Old Testament, God called David a man after His own heart (I Samuel 13:14). Often in his psalms David wrote of his desire to *dwell* in the presence of God.

Read Psalm 5:7-8 and 11-12. What is the benefit of taking refuge in God?

Read Psalm 18:1-3. Here David describes God's activity in nine ways, what are they?

1. _____ 2. _____ 3. _____

4. _____ 5. _____ 6. _____

7. _____ 8. _____ 9. _____

Face to Face with Jesus

The presence of God is a marvelous place! Would you sit at the feet of Jesus right now? Would you forget all your "to do list" and lose yourself in His presence?

Read Psalm 100 out loud.

Now read each verse and do as they say:

Verse 1: "**Shout** for joy!" Go ahead, let out a shout of praise! Lord, You are marvelous!

Verse 2: "Worship with gladness and joyful **singing.**" Sing a song of praise right now. (Don't worry how it sounds to you; sing to Him!)

Verse 3: **Know** the Lord is God. Thank Him for allowing you to be part of His flock.

Verse 4: Enter His gates with **thanksgiving.** Spend 3 minutes listing all the ways God has blessed you.

Verse 5: Read this verse out loud. List the 3 truths:

The Lord is _____.

His love endures _____.

His faithfulness continues through all _____.

MY PRAYER FOR TODAY

DAY 5
"MARY HAS CHOSEN WHAT IS BETTER"

Read Luke 10:38-42

Duty vs. Devotion

Martha's sense of duty drove her to set the necessary preparations in motion as soon as Jesus and His disciples arrived. She was understandably aggravated at Mary's absence. But when she asked Jesus to rebuke Mary for neglecting her duties, Jesus instead rebuked Martha! What would have happened if Martha hadn't fussed so over dinner?

> *Above all love each other deeply, because love covers a multitude of sins.*
> I Peter 4:8

Maybe everyone would have gone without dinner and to bed hungry. Maybe Jesus would have fed them two more fish and five more loaves! We'll never know.

The point is that when given the choice between having our service and having our undivided attention, Jesus chooses our undivided attention! He had been, is and always will be more interested in our hearts than our hands! And, He will reward our choice to nurture our love relationship with Him by being our defense in situations like this. Sometimes the "Marthas" of this world criticize those who choose spiritual devotion over religious duty! When Marthas are critical, Jesus will protect you from their fiery darts.

Meet God in His Word

Read Isaiah 26:3 and fill in the blanks.

You will keep in _____ _____ him

whose _____ is _____, because he

_____ in You.

Please hear me say, I am not suggesting that we become so heavenly minded that we are no earthly good! Nor am I suggesting that we let go all our responsibilities and replace them with Bible study and prayer. I am, however, suggesting that we spend enough time with Jesus to be saturated with the truth of John 15:5.

"I am the vine, you are the branches. If a man remains in me and I in him, he will bear much fruit; apart from me you can do nothing."

Jesus is the _____.

We are the _____.

What must we (the branches) do to bear much fruit? _____

_____

What can we do apart from Him? _____

Face to Face with Jesus

Jesus told Martha that the "abiding time" Mary was choosing far outweighed the working time Martha chose. *Choosing* to abide is an act of trust. By choosing to keep our heart-relationship strong through worship, Bible study and prayer, we are acknowledging our dependence on God to bear the fruit. By choosing quiet time *with* Him over hectic service *for* Him, we demonstrate our trust *in* Him to handle the details we can't!

Allow God to direct your thoughts as you answer these questions:

Are you more like Martha or Mary?

Is it ever necessary to be "in a tither" when you are walking with Jesus daily?

What is a sure sign of missing the "one thing" that is needed? (Luke 10:42)

Read Romans 15:13. What will God fill you with, as you trust in Him?

_____ and _____

When you trust in Him you will overflow with _____ by the power of the Holy Spirit.

Thank God for His trustworthiness. Agree with Him that you can do nothing apart from Him, and all things with Him!

MY PRAYER FOR TODAY

From the Hearts of Martha and Mary
(A story based on Luke 10:38-42)

Martha

When I heard they were coming I couldn't help but get excited. He's the most amazing man I've ever met! His very presence demands reverence and honor. Though He isn't wealthy, and the men who travel with Him are extremely common, He still carries Himself as one with great authority and power.

He's demonstrated that power many times. He heals the sick! Blind men see; crippled women walk straight. I've heard He even commands the wind and stops storms at sea. But the last time He was with us, He so focused His attention on us (Lazarus, my brother, Mary and me) that it was as if the rest of the world didn't matter.

I had been deeply affected by that visit. He'd said things that confused me, and I lay awake many nights turning His words over in my mind.

"Just believe!"

"Trust Me."

"Let not your heart be troubled."

I've never heard anyone say these things with such yearning. It was as if He knew that my decision to trust—or not to trust—was the most important decision of my life!

I wanted to honor Him with a feast fit for a king. I sent the servants to meet Him and invite Him into our home. As soon as they left, I started getting things in order. The rugs were spread, the dishes cleaned. Where was Mary? I needed her desperately! When there was work to be done, Mary always disappeared. After asking the servants if they'd seen her, she finally entered the outer courtyard coming back from the meadow behind our house. She carried a lovely bouquet of freshly cut flowers, I'll grant you that, but her face was shrouded in a dreamy mist.

"What's the matter with you?!" I shouted, too harsh I know, but for heaven's sake, why is she always out picking daisies when I'm home working?

"Oh, Martha, the birds are singing so loud this morning! It's as if they are heralding the coming of a king!" Mary answered my sharp demand with her typical gentle reply.

"Well, I've no time for birds and daisies. Jesus is coming and there is work to do!"

With that said, Mary immediately rushed to find vases for her flowers; she was convinced Jesus and His disciples desperately *needed* them in the gathering room when they arrived. Did she consider the fact that they might also need clean water to wash their feet, cold wine for their parched throats, or cheeses and fruit for refreshment after their long journey? No—not Mary; never does she ponder the practical needs of men, only the romantic notion that fresh flowers will make the perfect gift for a bunch of road-weary, hungry travelers. Mary is a hopeless romantic!

When Jesus arrived, I hardly had time to greet Him, there was so much work to do. Everything needed to be just right! Mary and I quickly ushered them into the largest room of our house. Proudly I offered servants with cool water and soft towels for bathing sore feet. I motioned for Mary to come with me to help with the wine we'd chilled in the brook. Once again Mary ignored my signal. By the time I set the goblets on the tray my temper was flaring!

I rushed back into the room with a tray full of cold drinks. His disciples thanked me, but I barely heard them, I was so angry with her. Jesus was laughing, talking and seeming to relax in our comfortable home. I was thrilled to offer Him this comfort considering His constant travel and unending confrontations with the synagogue rulers.

My contentment was quickly erased by Mary's gentle laugh. There she sat, not a care in the world, soaking in His every word. In a huff I nearly shouted, "Lord, don't You care that my sister has left me to do the work by myself? Tell her to help me!"

Immediately a hush came over the room. The disciples stopped talking to hear how Jesus would respond to me. There was an uncomfortable silence. I felt the blood rush to my cheeks. I wished I could erase the anger in my voice, but it was too late.

Jesus calmly looked at me. Every time I looked into His eyes I was caught up in a sea of compassion. The depth of His unchanging love drew me in. I wanted to cry, laugh and disappear all at the same time.

"Martha, Martha, you are worried and upset about so many things, but only one thing is needed. Mary has chosen what is better, and it will not be taken away from her."

Tears clouded my eyes. A lump swelled in my throat. Everyone was looking at me. I was hurt by His rebuke, but His words struck deep. I remembered how He looked my way during His last visit. He was explaining how His Father longed to have a personal relationship with each one of us. He'd answered someone's question: "Lord, how can we be part of this kingdom you describe?" He'd gently explained that in order to enter His kingdom we must consider the deep mysteries of our hearts. We must love God and love one another. That was when He looked at me.

With that look He'd said, "Martha, you need to consider your motives. What drives you to perform?" I knew He was saying this. For He knew I was preoccupied with activity. He knew I prided myself on what I could accomplish to keep my household running smoothly. He knew I was burdened by a reputation I had to fulfill!

Right there, in front of all our guests, my pride was stripped from me. Mary actually looked concerned and confused as I ran out of the room. I left the dinner. I don't even know if they ate that night. I went alone to the meadow—the same one that Mary had visited this morning when she returned with her flowers. At first I ran wildly, blinded by tears of rage and shame. I was still furious with Mary. It was all her fault! But, gradually the tears were exhausted, and I collapsed on the cool grass in the middle of the daisies. I caught a glimpse of a firefly. I lay on my back. The grass was damp and it smelt fresh and new. A dog howled in the distance. I looked up at the sky and saw a million twinkling lights.

What an amazing sight—the smells, the sounds, the stars twinkling. I sighed and giggled at the contrast between this place and what might have been going on in the kitchen due to my absence. As I thought about the depth of love I saw in His eyes, I realized His rebuke was meant to rescue me, not to condemn me.

And rescue me, He did.

Mary

Martha had been upset with me all day. I knew I aggravated her, but really she worried enough for *both* of us! With her "fussing" there was not a whole lot for me to do. Anytime I tried to help she seemed even more disgusted with me. I could never get the dishes clean enough, the fruit arranged just right or the rugs placed down in the exact spot. How the two of us could be so different is beyond me!

When Jesus and His disciples arrived, I had every intention of greeting them then graciously taking my leave to help with the meal. But I couldn't get away. His words were so full of mystery! Ever since His last visit I'd longed to hear more about His kingdom and its wonder. I longed for more and more of the love that seemed to flow in His presence. I felt like I was a thirsty doe drinking freely of soul-quenching water.

I barely even heard Martha's complaint. I was so caught up in the beauty of this coming kingdom. But His response to her complaint still rings in my ears: "Mary has chosen what is better, and it will not be taken from her."

Most likely I will never have the administrative skills Martha has. I'll never be able to make a roast that tastes the way her roast tastes. I will always be known as Martha's little sister. But the joy, peace and strength I find in the presence of Jesus will never, no not ever, be taken from me!

Questions for Reflection

1. Based on I Peter 4:8, what is the one thing that is most necessary?

2. What does it take to experience intimacy in a relationship?

3. Martha "worried about so many things." Do you? What things worry you?

4. How did Mary's calm assurance that Jesus would take care of things at the marriage feast illustrate her confidence in Him?

5. What things do you "do" *for* God? What does I Corinthians 13 say about these things?

6. Is it ever necessary to be in a "tither" when you are walking with Jesus daily?

7. According to Isaiah 26:3, how do we demonstrate to God that we trust Him?

8. What does God offer to those who trust Him?

Ask God To

- Take your worries and transform them into faith.
- Increase your love for Him and others.
- Be blessed by your willingness to trust in Him.

MY PRAYER FOR THIS WEEK

A VERSE TO MEMORIZE

I, the Lord, am your God,
Who brought you up from the land of Egypt;
Open your mouth wide and I will fill it.

—

Psalm 81:10

CHAPTER 2

True Satisfaction

WOMAN TOUCHED BY JESUS
The Woman at the Well
John 4

INTRODUCTION
"I Can't Get No Satisfaction!"

Chocolate, java, aromatherapy, massages, and diamonds—all these things are *supposed* to offer you satisfaction! Two days after my 40th birthday, I took my first cruise vacation (hopefully the first of many!). It was a gift from our church for my husband's 40th birthday (and it happened to embark just after I hit the big 4-0). Never had I kerplopped in such a large comfy lap of luxury! Lemon-ginger salt scrub and aromatherapy back massage, a French manicure, sea breezes, shopping, sun-bathing, fine dining, pizza anytime you want it, and ice cream *free*!

When I wrote this I was on a small plane flying from Ft. Lauderdale to Nashville returning home. Here's what I said: My climb out of that cozy lap and back into the hustle and bustle of motherhood, helpmate and ministry is a bumpy ride over a weather pattern cloaking Georgia. Like most luxuries the world has to offer, they all eventually come to an end.

However, many of us continue, "looking for love in all the wrong places." We seek satisfaction in things that promise but fail to deliver. The woman at the well had an encounter with Jesus that answered the mystery of true satisfaction.

What if we could be released from our futile search for happiness? What if we didn't have to buy the latest wrinkle-reducing skin creams, and we weren't snookered into purchasing yet another women's magazine that shouts at us in the cashier's line—"10 Days to Thinner Thighs" and "100 Ways to Enjoy Your Chocolate" printed over a luscious-looking 1200 calorie/85 fat gram serving of Granny Smith's Apple Delight dripping with cinnamon-hazelnut ice cream?

The woman at the well will carry us on a path of freedom, away from the false pleasures of this world and into the truly satisfying abundance that Jesus offers.

DAY 1
IMAGINARY LINES DRAWN BY PREJUDICE

Read John 4:1-9

Jews Despised Samaritans

Many devout Jewish travelers avoided Samaria on their journeys to and from Jerusalem. The Jews despised Samaritans. They were considered lesser in significance and beneath them in social standing. The enmity between Jews and Samaritans was deep with strong historical roots twisted throughout both their histories. By the time Jesus and His disciples traveled through Samaria, Jewish people considered Samaritan food as unclean as swine's skin (p. 747, the *Zondervan Pictorial Bible Dictionary* by Merrill C. Tenney, 1967).

> *I, the Lord, am your God,*
> *Who brought you up*
> *from the land of Egypt;*
> *Open your mouth wide*
> *and I will fill it.*
> Psalm 81:10

So, for Jesus to send His disciples to get something to eat, while He rested at the well was completely foreign to the disciples. However, this story proves that class structure, cultural norms and ethnic prejudice didn't matter one iota to Jesus. He was not bound by years of hatred. Jesus loved people, all people regardless of their ethnic background, occupation or social position. He was neither impressed nor was He depressed by a person's accomplishments or lack thereof. And since Jesus' love for people has no boundaries, the imaginary lines drawn around a land called Samaria never existed for Him.

Meet God in His Word

Imagine Jesus sitting by that well when the Samaritan woman approached Him. What might you have thought if you'd been her?

Jesus loved people regardless of their ethnic background, occupation or social position. What about you? Do you allow Jesus to love people through you today? What prejudices might you harbor? List them in the space provided.

Jesus was neither impressed nor depressed by a person's accomplishments or lack thereof. Are you caught in the deception that you must "perform" or "achieve" for God? In what ways do you try to gain God's approval?

Face to Face with Jesus

Those of us who were in church as little children learned this simple song. If you know the tune, sing it aloud now. If you don't know the tune, read the words and let God minister to your heart.

"Jesus loves the little children, all the children of the world. Red and yellow, black and white, they are precious in His sight. Jesus loves the little children of the world."

In many parts of our world, we've heard that there are countries "closed to the gospel." Perhaps the official word is that these countries are hostile to the gospel of Jesus Christ. Religious freedom does not exist, and Christians living there are tortured and sometimes martyred for their faith. But Jesus will go anywhere He pleases, and He will send His people—men and women willing to partner their hearts with His in these places. Some very brave Christians follow Jesus into these lands. Some very courageous Christians proclaim the name of Jesus in these countries, and many suffer torture and death for the sake of Christ. Because of their courage, these countries are not "closed to the gospel."

We need to pray for and support these bold efforts on behalf of the kingdom! Voice of the Martyrs provides free newsletters to anyone who wants to pray for the persecuted church. You can subscribe to their newsletter by visiting their website at www.persecution.com or by calling or writing them at their US office, phone: (918) 337-8015, fax: (918) 338-0189, address: P.O. Box 443, Bartlesville, OK 74005. You may also learn more about praying for and supporting missionaries by visiting the International Mission Board website at www.imb.org, or by calling 1-800-866-3621. Other missions' websites that might interest you are:

Youth With a Mission at www.ywam.org

Southern Baptist Woman's Missionary Union at www.wmu.com

Campus Crusade for Christ at www.ccfi.org

Ask God to take away imaginary lines of prejudice that years of subtle cultural influence have placed in you. Ask God to allow you to see and love people as He sees and loves them.

MY PRAYER FOR TODAY

DAY 2
LIVING WATER

Read John 4:1-9

Free Offers

Tom and I often receive "free" vacations in the mail. They are always to some exotic place absolutely or almost absolutely free! You just have to call, book your flight and talk to a vacation counselor within 48 hours to claim your "free" gift. We never have time to take these trips, and even if we did I'm sure there would be a "catch" somewhere. We would have to take a 90-minute tour and say "no, thank you" at least a dozen times to keep from purchasing some time-share week at the beach for the exceptionally low price of $9,999 with a low annual maintenance fee of $495 (guaranteed not to increase the first year), and then we would walk away with our "free gift" (dinner for two at some neighborhood restaurant).

> I, the Lord, am your God,
> Who brought you up
> from the land of Egypt;
> Open your mouth wide
> and I will fill it.
> Psalm 81:10

Nothing is free! Everything costs! Perhaps Samaritan society was much the same as ours. Perhaps the reason this woman was going to the well in the middle of the day was because she was an object of scorn amongst Samaritans. The woman at the well was so low on her social ladder that she had to stretch her arms high and stand on her tippy toes to reach the bottom rung. Jews hated Samaritans, and even Samaritans despised loose women. So, when Jesus offered something as enticing as "living water" (just the kind of water she'd been seeking for years), His offer seemed certain to hold some hidden agenda—there had to be strings attached somewhere.

Meet God in His Word

Read verse 7 again. Jesus was tired and _____.

Read verses 8-10. Jesus wasn't the only one thirsty. The Samaritan woman had a different kind of thirst, a thirst that went far deeper than physical thirst.

Have you experienced this thirst? Can you describe it in the space provided below?

Read verse 11. Where do you suppose this skepticism came from? Do you recall the last time you were offered a free gift? What is often attached to "free" gifts?

Read verses 11-15. What kind of water was Jesus offering? _____

_____

At this point, do you think the woman had moved beyond thinking of the water in the well? Support your answer with phrases from these verses:

Face to Face with Jesus

Are you ever guilty of allowing God to only penetrate the surface of your life? Do you bring Him shallow concerns? Are you too easily satisfied with a little worship, a little prayer, and a little fellowship with a few little Christian friends?

Jesus was not interested in the Samaritan woman's physical thirst. She had a dipper; she could reach into Jacob's well and get herself a drink of water. Jesus was interested in matters of the heart.

God is still interested in matters of the heart. In too many churches, too many Christians are satisfied with too little of what God has to offer. They limp along in defeat and depression carefully avoiding the crowd at the well, seeking solace in their misery and choosing to argue "religion" rather than open their mouths wide and receive what their spirits long to experience. God wants to introduce you to His abundant mercy, grace, compassion and love.

Psalm 81:10 says, *"I, the Lord, am your God. Open your mouth wide and I will fill it."*

Ask God to fill you with His living water today.

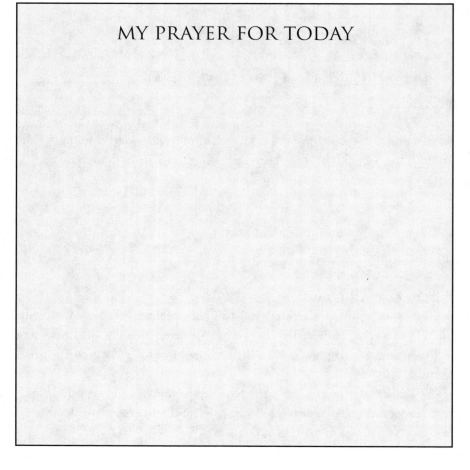

MY PRAYER FOR TODAY

DAY 3
PAINFULLY HONEST

Read John 4:13-18

The World's Fountain of Love

I had a friend once who was deeply in love with her third husband. She and he both had children from their two previous marriages. They gave a whole new definition to the blended family! I was blessed by their friendship as they chose to participate in the life of our church. They grew as a family, and sought to live pleasing to God. But they were under the burden of many difficulties related to the consequences of their life choices. They struggled through the complications of ex wives and husbands. They also struggled financially. Eventually they stopped coming to church and drifted from the atmosphere of a healthy faith family.

> I, the Lord, am your God,
> Who brought you up
> from the land of Egypt;
> Open your mouth wide
> and I will fill it.
> Psalm 81:10

While my friend was still married, she met and dated what she considered a "godly" man. Only, he too was still married. Once their affair was discovered and her third marriage was coming unglued, she called me in tears. She cried about life's cruelty. She cried because her father was an alcoholic and homeless. She cried because her mother depended on her to provide stability. She cried because she was hopelessly in love with a married man, and she cried because she'd hurt her own husband, the man she thought she loved only months before. She cried because she was still thirsty after she'd drunk time and again from the world's fountain of love. After all those husbands and boyfriends, she'd found that the world's fountain of love offered only bitter water made salty by endless tears.

Jesus knew the desperation and pain that resulted from trying desperately to dip love out of the world's deceptive fountain. So He confronted the woman at the well with the futility of that. God does that. One of the roles of the Holy Spirit is to confront us with sin. If you stay in His presence, and invite His scrutiny, He will boldly stand before you and sometimes carefully, sometimes abruptly (as in this situation) ask an incredibly difficult question and wait patiently for you to answer His inquiry.

Meet God in His Word

When Jesus offered "living water," what was the woman's response? (vv. 13-15)

"Sir, give me this water so that I won't get thirsty and have to _____

_____."

Read verses 16-18. Why do you suppose Jesus asked about her husband?

How many husbands had she had? _____ What about the man she lived with now?

What does this tell you about the woman at the well?

Face to Face with Jesus

Have you ever experienced the conviction of the Holy Spirit? What was your initial response to the Holy Spirit's conviction?

How did you feel when you yielded to the Holy Spirit's power as He convicted you of sin?

Read Psalm 81:6-10

The Lord promises to relieve our shoulders of the burden of sin. He promises to free our hands from the heavy basket of sin's labor. He tells us that when we call to Him out of our trouble, He will rescue us! How does God accomplish this rescue? Carefully read verse 8. The NASB version says,

"Hear, O My people, and I will *admonish* you."

God rescues you by *admonishing* you! When the Holy Spirit convicts you of sin, He does so to "rescue" you. Look closely at Psalm 81:8-16 and see how you receive the "living water" Jesus promised the woman at the well.

You shall have no foreign gods among you. (v. 9)
If my people would but listen to me (vv. 11, 13)
If Israel would follow my ways (v. 13)

Look at what is promised to us if we would have no other gods before our God, listen to God and follow His ways!

Open wide your mouth and *I will fill it.* (v. 10)
How quickly would I *subdue their enemies and turn my hand against their foes.* (v. 14)
But you would be *fed with the finest of wheat; with honey from the rock I would satisfy you.* (v. 16)

Don't you want to experience this spring of living water ever flowing from inside you? Don't you want to open wide your mouth and let God fill it?

This picture reminds me of baby birds. They sit helpless in their nest (provided by their parents) and chirp continually with their mouths wide open. All the while the mother and father birds search for the right food, secure this food, bring it safely back to the nest, and then place it in those wide-open mouths. As soon as the little birds get one mouth full, they start all over again.

God wants us to be like those baby birds. He wants us to receive His conviction, swallow our pride and feast on the healthy fare of humility. He wants us to desperately open our mouths wide, chirp with all our hearts, and wait for His perfect provision for us. Let God fill your wide-open mouth today.

MY PRAYER FOR TODAY

DAY 4
RELIGION VS. RELATIONSHIP

Read John 4:19-24

Staying "Safe"

"Sir," the woman said, "I can see that you are a prophet.
Our fathers worshiped on this mountain, but you Jews claim
that the place where we must worship is in Jerusalem."
John 4:19-20

What a classic example of trying to divert attention! Jesus marched right past a shallow encounter and penetrated her heart! When the Holy Spirit *admonishes* us, it often hurts. Emotions are stirred in spite of our gallant efforts to tuck them safely away. So, like the woman at the well we often try to divert attention to easier, safer subjects. The woman at the well chose religion.

Many people find safety in "religion." They find security in "religion." They attend church on Sunday mornings, enjoy the singing and the preaching, then walk away with their religious activity checked off their "to do" list. Then they go about their daily lives with no further thought toward God.

> *I, the Lord, am your God,*
> *Who brought you up*
> *from the land of Egypt;*
> *Open your mouth wide*
> *and I will fill it.*
> Psalm 81:10

God doesn't want religious people! When Jesus walked on the earth His greatest adversaries were religious people! Jesus spoke His sharpest words to the religious leaders of the day. Religion is easily twisted into meaningless activity that poses as an imposter to true RELATIONSHIP with God. God longs for relational people—not religious people.

Meet God in His Word

How did Jesus answer the woman's attempt at a religious argument? Carefully read verses 23-24 again. Jesus defined true worshipers as those who worship Him in

_____ and in _____

How do we worship God in spirit and in truth?

Worship is too often identified by music. God intends for worship to be so much more than musical style! Music is often part of worship because God created us to be touched deeply through melody. Music comforts (such as David's harp playing when Saul was tormented by spirits); music energizes and strengthens us (that's why the musicians went first into battle). Music causes us to reflect, relax and focus. But music alone is not worship.

Worship happens when we draw ourselves carefully away from the frantic lives we lead and focus on the object of our affection. Genuine worship happens when all our affection focuses on God. Worship requires action on our part.

The Bible describes worship with action words.

Read the following passages of Scripture and circle the action words you find:

Psalm 100 • Psalm 105:1-6 2 • Chronicles 5:11-14
Romans 12:1-2

Shout • Sing • Know • Enter His Gates • Give Thanks • Praise Him •
Make Known • Tell • Glory • Seek • Withdraw •
Consecrate Yourself • Remember • Renew Your Mind • Look •
Stand • Offer Yourself • Be Transformed

There are examples in the Bible of kneeling, bowing, laying prostrate, jumping, leaping, dancing, crying...of worshiping God in spirit and in truth!

In my church today, where my husband serves as pastor, we experience freedom in our worship services. We cry, raise our hands, bow, stand, sit and some even dance. There have been powerful "sermons" preached through the authentic worship of our congregation. Through our willingness to engage our bodies and our hearts with our spirits in worship, we receive enormous outpourings of the power of God. Many people come to know

Jesus through our worship service ministry, and our church continues to grow at an accelerated rate. But if our worship were to end at the conclusion of those services, we would fall far short of living lives of genuine worship for God. We also must engage in the same devotion that commits our lives to service in God's Kingdom work through the ministries our church offers our community and the world.

Face to Face with Jesus

God is looking for children who would worship Him in spirit and in truth. Try to find some time today to allow God to take you on a journey of reflection. Record the many ways He's loved you and worship Him in spirit and in truth.

> "I, the Lord, am your God, Who brought you up from
> the land of Egypt. Open your mouth wide and I will fill it."
> Psalm 81:10

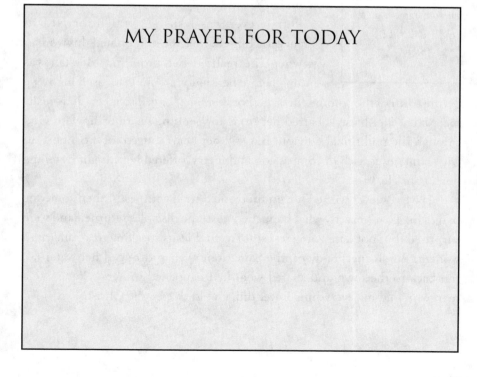

MY PRAYER FOR TODAY

DAY 5
OPEN WIDE YOUR MOUTH,
AND I WILL FILL IT

Read John 4:25-42

Hope in a Savior

Just after Jesus urged the woman at the well to move past ritual and religion, she then opened her heart wide and shared her heart's desire with Jesus. "I know that Messiah (called Christ) is coming. When He comes, He will explain everything to us" (John 4:25 NIV).

Apart from insignificant details of religious activity (such as *where* to worship), the woman declared her hope that one day the Messiah would come. She told Jesus also that when He came, He would make all things right! He would explain all things!

> *I, the Lord, am your God,*
> *Who brought you up*
> *from the land of Egypt;*
> *Open your mouth wide*
> *and I will fill it.*
> Psalm 81:10

Jesus was touched by her hope in the coming Messiah. Immediately He told her, "I who speak to you am he."

Rarely ever was Jesus so straightforward in reference to Himself. Imagine how excited this woman was when she realized her promised Messiah was standing before her! For years she'd focused her hope on the truth of the coming Messiah. For years she longed to meet God—really meet Him. Her lifestyle barred her from any genuine relationship with God through the traditional religion. But still her heart longed for a connection with Him. Jesus, rich in compassion and mercy, offered her insight by telling her, "I am He."

Have you ever wished for uninterrupted time with Jesus, then someone barges in? That's exactly what happened next: the disciples returned and were surprised (but not dare going to say so) to find Jesus speaking to a Samaritan woman. But at that moment, the Samaritan woman dropped her water jar, ran back to the town and shared what had happened to her, "Come, see a man who told me everything I ever did. Could this be the Christ?"

Meet God in His Word

Why did she leave her water jar behind?

_____

Based on the fact that the woman went to the well at an odd time of the day, what is unusual about her actions when she returned to town?

_____

Don't forget that this woman was not considered a "nice" woman. She most likely went to the well in the middle of the day because she wanted to avoid the other women. They probably shunned her and shut her out of their kitchen gadget and jewelry parties. But, after meeting Jesus, and hearing Him declare Himself the Messiah, she ran back to town and immediately went to everyone she used to avoid, so she could tell them about Him.

This exciting encounter affected Jesus and the woman in a physical as well as a spiritual way. Physical needs and concerns took a backseat to spiritual matters. God was at work and Jesus was excited about joining Him. God was at work and the woman at the well didn't stay there!

Read verses 31-38. What did Jesus say His food was? (look in v. 34)

_____

Jesus knew Samaria was about to experience revival. He was so excited about their coming salvation that His physical hunger took a backseat to His spiritual anticipation. The woman at the well was so moved by Jesus' ability to penetrate her heart with His love and power that she was no longer thirsty. So, both Jesus and the woman at the well moved beyond physical concerns to focus instead on spiritual ones. In the verses you just read, Jesus was inviting; no deeper than that, He was _urging_ His disciples to do the same.

At the very moment that Jesus said, "open your eyes and look at the fields," Samaritans might have been pouring out of town coming toward them at Jacob's well. Maybe the disciples could see them coming by the hundreds as they followed Jesus' glance.

Read verse 39 and fill in the blanks:

_____ of the Samaritans from the town _____ in Him because of the _____ testimony.

God used the cold, crusty heart of a sinful woman to usher a great move of His Spirit among the people. Samaritans who responded to the woman's testimony came to meet Jesus. They urged Him to change His travel plans, and rather than pass right through their town, they invited Jesus to stay with them for a few days. Jesus stayed two more days in Samaria. The Holy Spirit opened the eyes of the Samaritans and verse 41 tells us "many more became believers."

Verse 42 provides a beautiful summary to this story. The same men and women who previously shut this woman out thanked her for sharing Jesus with them. "We no longer believe just because of what you said, now we have heard for ourselves, and we know that this man really is...

...the Savior of the world."

Face to Face with Jesus

Do you remember how glorious it was to first realize "Jesus is the Savior of the world"? Or, even better than that, to realize the same Jesus who saved the world longed to save you, too? Would you be willing to give up your physical concerns for spiritual ones, perhaps for a day (or even one meal)? Consider giving up a meal today, and instead of eating, spend some time talking with God. Ask Him where He's working in your world and join Him there.

MY PRAYER FOR TODAY

From the Heart of the Woman at the Well
(A story based on John 4)

I actually slept late that day. Jonas was slow to get up; he's not too motivated to work. I'm not sure where he gets the coins we spend on food. After preparing his breakfast, I wrapped my shawl around my head and went outside to get the water jar. I thought I heard my neighbors giggling. Rebecca's wedding ceremony will be any day now, and there's so much activity over there. I remember my first wedding. Back then I, too, was surrounded by girl friends and family.

I don't know what went wrong. Andrew just wasn't a good choice, I guess. My father didn't really care. He just wanted me married because that's what girls do. Andrew didn't love me. My mother said we would learn to love each other like she and my father did. I'm not sure they ever really learned to love each other. I never saw much affection between them.

Andrew and me, we were young. Affection? We had that! Or, maybe it was just lust; I'm not sure I even know the difference.

When he divorced me, my life was over. All my friends acted as if I didn't exist. My parents even believed the lies that I had slept with other men. How could they? Of course, I didn't!

Well, do you have to count Saul? He was so kind and considerate. Where Andrew was demanding and sullen, Saul was fun and...so...romantic. It was mischievous, I know...OK, not only mischievous, that's too innocent a word for what we did. I know it was sin, pure sin. (Not that it wasn't fun, mind you.) But Saul also turned out to be wrong for me.

After my divorce from Andrew, I tried to hide my shame in Saul's robe. I guess Andrew could have had me stoned, but even though they didn't actually toss rocks at me, I died a slow suffocating death by their shunning.

It didn't take long for the excitement of stealing intimate moments with Saul to fade away. Just like the mist that rises in the evening and evaporates in the daylight, so Saul's love for me seemed to vanish into thin air. He tired quickly of my moaning about having no friends. And he simply wasn't capable of being a friend, lover, provider, a rock of strength and refuge. I guess it was too much for him. So, he left me, too.

Of course, it didn't hurt as much that time. I'd been there before. Then my hopeless search for life and meaning in relationships took me on various excursions with Judas, Silas and Thad. None of them lasted. Wasn't there anyone out there who could love me? Wasn't there anyone out there who cared? Was it ever possible to have a love relationship that could last forever?

I gave up on marriage. Too much trouble with too much legality. Jonas and I would just by-pass all those rules and live together. He was OK, I guess. But already I could feel the pattern of passion, disdain, arguments, hopelessness and abandonment beginning to return. This morning my mind was dull, and my heart was numb as I heard the giggles grow silent. With my jar carefully balanced on my head I focused my eyes on the path and held my chin up when I walked past the girls. I felt their stares and heard their whispers though they thought I wasn't listening.

I saw Him sitting by the well and almost went back home to come again later. But I knew that if I went back, the girls would still be outside playing, and they'd wonder why I didn't have water in my jar. It was already late in the day, and I'd already hauled my jar up the hill; so why should I leave empty handed simply to avoid this one man? At least it was a man and not a mean old woman.

I tried not to make eye contact with Him, although I was curious as to why a Jewish man might be sitting alone by this well. Jewish people avoided Samaria just like Samaritans avoided me! I set my jar down and lowered the dipper to draw my water, hoping to get the job done quickly and be on my way.

Then He spoke, "Will you give Me a drink?"

Pardon? Did you say something to me? I must be more winded than I thought...because Jewish men do not talk to Samaritan women. They don't even acknowledge our existence!

What did you say? "Will you give Me a drink?"

"You are a Jew, and I am a Samaritan woman. How can you ask me for a drink?" I didn't mean for my voice to sound so sharp; but after years of snubbing by my family, neighbors and friends, I was not in the mood for some set up by a Jew! Why didn't he just leave me alone?

But instead, He answered me, "If you knew the gift of God and who it is that asks you for a drink, you would have asked Him and He would have given you living water."

Now I thought He'd had too much sun! What on earth was He talking about? Men had promised me too many things too many times.

"I'll give you security, a family and a home," Andrew had whispered.

"I'll give you the moon!" Saul promised.

"I'll take you as you are, I'll love you till the day we die, I do, I will, I can't, I'm sorry, I couldn't ...too bad."

"Sir," I tried to sound kinder this time, His voice was so full of—what was it? Could it be compassion? "Sir, you have nothing to draw with, and this well—well, sir, this well is deep!"

Kind of like my heart. Deep and filled with remorse, regret, pain and emptiness.

"Where can you get this living water? Are you greater than our father Jacob, who gave us the well and drank from it himself, as did also his sons and his flocks and herds?" I wanted this Jewish man to know that I was familiar with our shared heritage. He needed to know that He was not dealing with an ignorant woman here!

Then, He said the strangest thing, "Everyone who drinks this water will be thirsty again, but whoever drinks the water I give him will never thirst. Indeed, the water I give him will become in him a spring of water welling up to eternal life."

Whoa. How could He know so much about me?

Water...we're talking about water here.

That's all He knows...water.

...living water...

Oh to have the thirst in my heart quenched for once and for all!

Love...deep abiding, perfect, ever-flowing, abundant love!

How I longed for its cool embrace!

Living water, welling up in me!

But, we're talking about water here! I'm at a well, He's asking for a drink, and He is a Jewish man who is speaking riddles to me!

"Sir, give me this water so that I won't get thirsty and have to keep coming here to draw water." (Let's see if He can deliver!)

I looked Him in the eyes. This was the first time I'd looked in His eyes. Looking back at me were deep pools of what looked like the most desirable living water I could imagine. Suddenly I was thirsty for whatever He had that filled those eyes with such perfect love. I cannot even describe them to you.

He captured me in His eyes and held me in their firm embrace. Then without judgment or contempt, but with honesty and authority, He said, "Go, call your husband and come back."

I couldn't take my eyes off Him. I swallowed hard. Although I had this eerie feeling He knew this already, I trembled as I barely whispered, "I have no husband."

He didn't even blink, still wrapping His complete acceptance around my quivering heart as I bathed in the compassion of His eyes; He spoke slowly, "You are right when you say you have no husband. The fact is, you have had five husbands, and the man you now have is not your husband. What you have just said is quite true." After He said it, He released me momentarily by looking toward the town.

I stood still, wondering how He could know all that. Who was this? And what did He want with me?

"Sir, I can see that you are a prophet." I then tried to engage Him in a religious discussion. That was safer. No more talking about me and my personal life; let's talk about something else. Why not trigger a debate, let's see what He thinks of our age-old dispute.

With skill in answering religious diversions, He quickly brought the subject right back around to put my heart front and center again. "Woman, a time is coming when you will worship the Father neither on this mountain nor in Jerusalem...God is spirit, and His worshipers must worship in spirit and in truth."

Spirit and truth.

What *is* truth?

I'd hidden from it so long the depths of my heart couldn't even go there. Too much pain, too many broken promises, too much regret. I felt like my heart was laid bare before Jehovah Himself. How could this man penetrate me with those eyes then pierce me with His words? How could He know all about my husbands and my failed attempts at love? Why did I feel completely exposed and totally unafraid at the same time?

Who are you?

"I know that Messiah is coming. When He comes, He will explain everything to us." I tried to sound brave as I said it. When I spoke these words I searched for truth in His eyes. I was baiting Him; I wondered, just maybe, could He be? My heart thumped hard against my chest. My hands trembled.

Who are you? Could you be...?

If you are...is this what love is?

Why me?

Why would I, after all my completely failed life...

How would I be so honored that you would reveal yourself to me?

I almost knew what He was going to say before He even said it,

"I, who speak to you am He."

YES!

I knew it! I knew it.

I knew in my heart it was Him.

I couldn't speak. Immediately my mind opened wide with wonder and awe. I could literally feel the layers of rejection and failure peel away from my cold heart, and sense it thaw like the snow when spring's sun melts away the chill. I rejoiced in the sense of love coursing through every fiber of my being. Love rushing like a river into the joints and marrow of my bones.

Soon there were other men all around; they must have been His disciples, I don't remember acknowledging their presence. I completely forgot my water jar and ran back toward town, energized by this river of life pressing me on. The faster I ran, the stronger the river flowed, healing the tears, rips, jagged corners and impossibly destroyed tissues of my soul in its strong current of love. By the time I arrived at the marketplace, a brand new heart beat strong in my spirit!

The old things were gone! Completely washed away in the flash flood of His forgiveness, gone...all my mistakes and failures, gone! All my hurt and shame, gone! God knew all about me and He loved me anyway!

Where once I was bound to sin, regret, and shame, now I was set free. I was free to talk to them, free to tell them, free to take them to Jesus. And they listened! Those same people who wouldn't look me in the eye, they listened, they went with me, and they met Jesus, too.

I picked up my water jar the other day. I'd forgotten it in my hurry. It was filled to the brim with the cleanest, coolest water I'd ever tasted. But even that water didn't compare to the spring of living water that wells up in my heart even now as I tell you this story. Jesus has come, and He is the Savior of the world!

Questions for Reflection

1. In what ways do you seek to satisfy the hunger in your heart and soul?

2. What does God promise to do for you in Psalm 81:10?

3. In what ways do you try to gain God's approval? Why is God neither impressed nor depressed by your actions?

4. Describe spiritual thirst.

5. What does conviction of sin feel like initially?

6. What does conviction of sin feel like when you yield to the Holy Spirit's power?

7. Describe what it means to worship in spirit and truth. Have you ever experienced such worship?

8. What did the Samaritan woman do that gave evidence to her inner change? What have you done that gives evidence of God's working in your heart?

Ask God To

- Allow you to have an intimate conversation with a woman you know who may be like the Samaritan woman.
- Use you to lead her to Jesus' living water.
- Be glorified in your own life as you leave this place and give outward expression to what He's done in your heart.

MY PRAYER FOR THIS WEEK

A VERSE TO MEMORIZE

*Humble yourself therefore under
the mighty hand of God that He may
exalt you at the proper time.*

—

2 Peter 5:6

CHAPTER 3

God's Path of Humility

WOMAN TOUCHED BY JESUS
The Woman Who Anointed Jesus
Matthew 26:6-13; Mark 14:1-10;
Luke 7:36-50; John 12:1-11

INTRODUCTION
Expressions of Love

When we were in middle school, girlfriends would giggle as they received top-secret messages from the cutest boys in the class. The one girl lucky enough to be the object of affection would open the carefully folded note and read: "I like you. Do you like me? Circle one: yes, no, or maybe."

Smiling discreetly at the boy, she would circle her response and choose a maiden to deliver the message. Or, she would poke her finger toward her mouth and roll her eyes in disgust.

Do you remember those days? Do you remember how it felt to send one of those notes? Ah, come on now, surely you sent at least one of those notes! If not, did you ever receive one? Did receiving someone's expression of adoration make your heart flip flop?

What tumultuous times we had when we were discovering how to express our affection. Even now, many adults have a difficult time giving and receiving love. Some people have a hard time feeling accepted because someone they loved chose to leave them. Some adults still have a hard time showing love toward others for fear of ridicule or rejection. What if you express your deep concern, love and devotion and they poke their finger toward their mouth and roll their eyes as their friends roar with laughter?

In this chapter, we're going to visit with a woman who poured her love on Jesus. She used perfume. Although her heart might have been racing and she might have been hurt by the men who basically poked their fingers in their mouths, rolled their eyes and laughed at her, she chose to vulnerably, humbly, express her love for Jesus.

The story of Jesus' encounter with this woman is recorded in all four gospels. In Matthew 26:6-13 and in Mark 14:1-10 the encounter took place in Bethany at the home of Simon the leper. The woman anointed Jesus' head with oil as He reclined at the table. Luke (7:36-50) wrote that Simon was a Pharisee and the woman poured the perfume over Jesus' feet after she bathed them with her tears. John (12:1-11) recorded the same story, but in his account Jesus met the woman in Bethany; only this time He was at Martha's home and Mary was the one who anointed Jesus' feet.

We're not going to worry about the details of the story. Instead we are going to focus on the fact that this woman (who had lived a sinful life) came into a room filled with men, broke an expensive alabaster jar and anointed Jesus with valuable oil of pure nard. Without concern for how she might be criticized, she focused her devotion on Jesus and worshipped Him in a vulnerable, costly way.

In order to follow her example, we must embrace humility. For us to experience God's love toward us and for us to express our love to Him, we must saturate ourselves with humility.

Humility is simply agreeing with God about two things:
1. Who He says we are.
2. Who He says He is.

DAY 1
PRIDE GOES BEFORE DESTRUCTION

Read Matthew 26:6-13

What Is Pride?

In order to better understand humility, let's look at its opposite: pride.

The New Merriam-Webster Dictionary defines pride as: conceit, justifiable self-respect, elation over an act or possession, haughty behavior, disdain, ostentatious display.

What does pride look like?

Pride puts *my* comfort, pleasure, relief, needs and *me* in the center of *my* thoughts. Pride thinks about *me* most of the time. Pride places *me* in the center of every situation, every circumstance and every relationship.

Pride is self-sufficient, either refusing help when it is offered or having an "I can do it me-self!" attitude. When my daughter Kaleigh was barely able to talk, she learned to say these words, "I can do it me-self!" She didn't want my help pulling her shirt over her head. She didn't need me to hold her hand. She didn't want me to spread jelly on her toast! Kaleigh is a lot like her mother. She has an independent streak that refuses to receive help when it's offered. Pride is the beast in our belly that roars, "I can do it me-self!"

> *Humble yourself therefore under the mighty hand of God that He may exalt you at the proper time.*
> 2 Peter 5:6

Pride says, "Nobody knows the trouble I've seen..." Pride tricks you into believing your hurt is worse, your pain is greater and your future is more hopeless than anyone else's.

Ecclesiastes 1:9 says, *"What has been will be again, what has been done will be done again, there is nothing new under the sun."* If ever you get stuck with this pride pressing you down, pinning you to the ground with the thought that "ain't nobody ever experienced the pain you've suffered," consider Job!

Pride refuses to recognize truth. Pride believes lies and gives into the deception of Satan. Pride relies on emotion and reason. Hear me say right now, we have no reason to rely on emotion! Our emotional self is our weakest, most unpredictable, shallow self! I can sit here and inhale the scent of my "apples 'n oak" candle fragrance and feel good. I can wake up in the morning with a headache and feel bad. If I choose to live according to my emotions, I will be a slave to Satan's deception.

Pride says, "If I can't do it...it can't be done."

Based on these descriptions, what does pride look like in you?

Several years ago, I read through the entire Old Testament with my son, TJ (he was six at the time). When we got to the place where the many kings ruled Israel, we saw a pattern emerge. God warned the king that He was the one who put the king on the throne. The king humbly received his position, mindful of God's authority over the nation. Eventually the people would so revere the king that the king would begin to believe he was the great ruler they told him he was. The king would then allow himself to indulge in the pleasures of his position and before long he'd disregard God's rules.

At this point in the story, one night TJ said, "Oh no, here we go again!" Because he knew that God was about to send someone to stab the king in his fat belly (TJ especially liked that story), or the king was about to fall over dead, or another foreign army was about to trounce the kingdom and leave the king powerless.

It never failed...pride went before a great fall.

Meet God in His Word

Proverbs 16:18 says, "Pride goes before destruction, a haughty spirit before a fall."

Look up the following verses and fill in the blanks to discover how God feels about pride:

- Proverbs 16:5 The Lord _____ all the proud.
- James 4:6 God _____ the proud but gives grace to the humble.
- Proverbs 8:13 I _____ pride and arrogance.

God is not neutral on the issue of pride. He does not sit by and allow pride to take up residence in your life. God actively opposes pride. He actively opposes the pride that is in you! God is against pride.

Why? Because pride blinds you to WHO GOD IS! This was the fatal flaw in the religious leaders of Jesus' day. Their pride could not allow them to see Jesus as the Messiah.

Pride is the opposite of humility.

Face to Face with Jesus

The woman who anointed Jesus with oil proceeded to pour her love over the head of Jesus even in the midst of criticism and hostility. She was not limited by thoughts such as these: What will they think of me? I'm not worthy! What if they speak harshly to me? Who do I think that I am?

Consider the subject of each of those thoughts. When you allow thoughts such as these to stifle your worship, you allow pride to choke your love for Christ. Has God revealed pride in you through the study today? If so, confess it right now. Admit it, ask God to forgive it, quit it and God will forget it!

MY PRAYER FOR TODAY

DAY 2
HUMILITY IS AGREEING
WITH GOD ABOUT
WHO HE SAYS WE ARE

Read Mark 14:1-9

What Is Humility?

Humility is simply agreeing with God about two things:

1. Who He says we are.
2. Who He says He is.

Yesterday we took a long hard look at pride. Today we'll consider humility. God takes great pleasure in reminding us of just how He sees us...lest we begin to be puffed up with *who* we think we are!

On Tuesday, September 17, 2002, I had a rather humbling experience. We were in the midst of closing on the house we'd just sold and the one we purchased. We signed the papers on our new house on Friday, we moved on Saturday and we were scheduled to close on our old house on the afternoon of the 17th.

> *Humble yourself therefore under the mighty hand of God that He may exalt you at the proper time.*
>
> 2 Peter 5:6

I was working for the TN Baptist Convention, and part of my job was to go into churches and speak to their women. On September 17 I'd been invited to speak at a church in East Nashville whose pastor was the president of the TN Baptist Convention. I remembered the closing but figured I could easily go speak to the women in the East Nashville church in the morning and be back in Franklin in plenty of time for our appointment.

However, I'd forgotten about Dr. Morris Chapman's 10th anniversary luncheon. Tom asked me to put September 17 on my calendar months before so I could join him at Dr. C's luncheon. Tom was going to pray as part of the program. Dr. Chapman is a member of our church and the executive director of the Southern Baptist Convention. Every leader of every Southern Baptist anything would be present at this luncheon. The seminary presidents, mission agency presidents, mega church pastors, state convention directors....anyone who was anybody in Southern Baptist life would be present at the luncheon. I'd forgotten to mark the date on my calendar. When I told Tom about my plans to go to East Nashville, he reminded me of the luncheon. Instead of cancelling my speaking engagement, I decided I could do both and still make our afternoon appointment at the attorney's office in Franklin to close on our house.

On Tuesday morning Tom and I both put on suits. Our children knew something was up because we don't normally dress up to go to work where our church sits across the street from a pig barn! They asked, "Where are you going today?" To which we explained that we would be attending a most prestigious luncheon. I have to admit, just the invitation to be there was somewhat impressive.

I knew my schedule would be tight, and all would have worked just fine, except that President Bush was also in Nashville for a luncheon that same day...in that same hotel! It was raining (of course...after all we were moving), and I was driving Tom's humble Honda. We call it that because Tom takes great pride in not having to have a new car. He chooses cars for their expression of humility. He's even been known to give away (or crash) his cars so he can purchase more humble cars. I on the other hand do not need that expression of humility. Nevertheless, I was driving Tom's humble Honda that day.

I was also one week away from a prayer retreat I coordinated for the TN Baptist Convention. We'd anticipated 200 women coming and over 500 registered. So, there were important papers and files and miscellaneous items related to the retreat that I didn't want to lose in our move. I placed all those things in the front seat of the Honda.

Since I arrived late to the hotel, I took advantage of valet parking. After I gave my keys to the attendant, I met my escort and hurried into the banquet room. Tom was mingling among the prominent masses. We were promptly ushered on stage to the head table—the one that faces everyone else. Tom prayed a lovely blessing over the food, and we thoroughly enjoyed the luncheon. I met some of the choicest people in Southern Baptist life, and we all visited as we went outside to wait for our cars. Lincolns, Cadillacs, Volvos...and one humble Honda came to be matched to their drivers. The air conditioning was not working on the Honda at this time, so even though it was raining, I had to unroll the windows to keep them from getting fogged. I waved "good bye" to the prominent wives of the prominent men and claimed my humble wheels.

The fee for valet parking cost more than the car was worth!

I offered Tom a ride back to where he'd parked his car. My good husband cannot comprehend the thought of paying someone else to park your car. So, he parked for free and walked the three blocks to the hotel. Because my car was so full of "important stuff" in the front seat, Tom had to take his place in the backseat. We loaded up, waved goodbye again and backed into the wet street. Tom mentioned how ridiculous we must look and we roared with laughter. Here we were, pastor and wife at cow patty Baptist church...pulling out of valet parking in our humble Honda where the only seat for him was in the back! What a sense of humor God has.

I was telling this story later to the women in my office later that day. They laughed with me, and as they walked out of my office, I reached around to my back because my skirt felt a little funny. At which time I realized all day long my skirt had been unzipped!

God takes great pleasure in reminding us of JUST how He sees us.

Meet God in His Word

Humility is agreeing with God about who He says we are. Read the following verses and circle the phrases that tell us who God says we are:

Psalm 103:14

". . . for He knows how we are formed, He remembers that we are dust."

Ephesians 2:1-3

"As for you, you were dead in your transgressions and sins, in which you used to live when you followed the ways of this world and of the ruler of the king-dom of the air, the spirit who is now at work in those who are disobedient. All of us also lived among them at one time, gratifying the cravings of our sinful nature and following its desires and thoughts. Like the rest, we were by nature objects of wrath."

Ephesians 2:8-10

"For it is by grace you have been saved, through faith—and this not from yourselves, it is the gift of God—not by works, so that no one can boast. For we are God's workmanship, created in Christ Jesus to do good works, which God prepared in advance for us to do."

We are His projects! I don't know about you, but when I have a project, it has me. My project receives my undivided attention. The success or failure of my project reflects who I am and what I'm capable of doing. We are God's projects! His undivided attention is on completing us in His image!

John 15:13-15

"Greater love has no one than this, that he lay down his life for his friends. You are my friends if you do what I command. I no longer call you servants, because a servant does not know his masters' business. Instead, I have called you friends, for everything that I learned from my Father I have made known to you."

2 Chronicles 16:9

We are God's treasures "for the eyes of the Lord range throughout the earth to strengthen those whose hearts are completely His."

Face to Face with Jesus

How did the woman who anointed Jesus with oil demonstrate her humility? How did her humility minister to Jesus?

Read Mark 14:10-11. Do you think Jesus' rebuke had any bearing on Judas' decision?

How did pride or humility play into Judas' demise?

Thank God for telling you how He sees you today. Choose one of the verses you read today, and allow it to encourage you as you go about your business of living a life of humility.

MY PRAYER FOR TODAY

DAY 3
HUMILITY IS AGREEING WITH GOD ABOUT WHO HE SAYS HE IS.

Read Luke 7:36-50

Whining

Yesterday we talked about who God says we are. Can you agree with who God says you are? Today we will dig deeper into God's understanding of who we are and then discover who He says He is.

To get started, I want you to whine. In the space provided I want you to tell God how pitiful you are. Take a look at your inadequacies, your burden, and the weight of your load. Psalm 103:14 tells us He's mindful we are merely dust; the problem is that we are not! We forget that we are merely dust!

> *Humble yourself therefore under the mighty hand of God that He may exalt you at the proper time.*
> 2 Peter 5:6

Whine:

Once Saint Francis of Assisi was confronted by a brother who asked him repeatedly, "Why you? Why you?"

Francis responded, in today's terms, "Why me what?"

"Why does everyone want to see you? Hear you? Obey you? You are not all that handsome, nor learned, nor from a noble family. Yet the world seems to want to follow you," the brother said.

Then Francis raised his eyes to heaven, knelt in praise to God, and turned to his interrogator:

"You know what? It is because the eyes of the Most High have willed it so. He continually watches the good and the wicked, and as His most holy eyes have not found among sinners any smaller man, nor any more insufficient and sinful, therefore He has chosen me to accomplish the marvelous work which God hath undertaken; He chose me because He could find none more worthless, and He wished to confound the nobility and grandeur, the strength, the beauty and the learning of this world."

(excerpt from *Spiritual Leadership* by Oswald Sanders, p. 30-31 The Moody Bible Institute, 1967, 1980, 1994 as quoting James Burns, *Revivals, Their Laws and Leaders*, p. 95 London: Hodder & Stoughton, 1909. The text in this quotation has been modernized.)

Look at your "whine." You've just qualified yourself to be truly great in God's kingdom service. He chooses to lift up the humble. You want to be lifted up? Get bowed down. Agree with God on who He says you are.

Meet God in His Word

Humility is also agreeing with God about who He says He is. Look up the following verses and print a phrase or phrases that tell what God reveals to us about Himself:

• Genesis 17:1

• Exodus 34:6-7

• Job 5:8-9

• Psalm 46:1

• Psalm 62

• John 6:35

- John 4:13-14

- John 14:6

Face to Face with Jesus
When has God been these things to you? Try to think of one example of Him demonstrating each of these character traits on your behalf.

Thank God for His reality in your life.

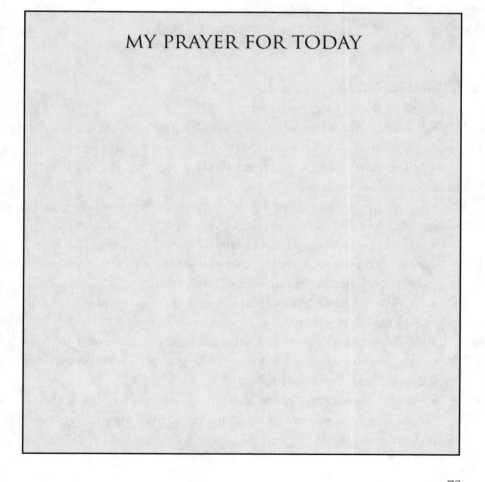

MY PRAYER FOR TODAY

DAY 4
HUMILITY IS SIMPLY AGREEING WITH GOD ABOUT TWO THINGS

Read Luke 7:36-50

To Be Loved by God

When the Pharisee thought to himself, "If only Jesus *knew* what kind of woman this is!" Jesus told the Pharisee about two men, both with a debt, one larger than the other. And when He asked the Pharisee which man would be more grateful for the canceled debt, the Pharisee admitted the man with the greater debt. But don't miss the fact that both men owed a debt...and both debts were forgiven.

> *Humble yourself therefore under the mighty hand of God that He may exalt you at the proper time.*
> 2 Peter 5:6

Consider the following statements:

• You will never experience God's salvation until you experience your desperation.

• You are never going to experience God's power until you come face to face with your weakness.

• You are not going to experience His compassion, His graciousness, His patience, love and faithfulness until you recognize your failure.

• You will not know God as Creator, Sustainer, Redeemer and Friend until He takes you beyond the end of yourself and into a place where His redemption is the only thing that keeps you afloat.

• You will not know Him as your refuge and strength...an ever-present help in time of trouble until you find yourself in trouble!

• He will not be your rock—your salvation, your mighty fortress in whose tender care you will not be shaken—as long as you can maintain your stability in your own strength.

• Jesus is not your bread of life, your living water, the way, the truth and the life as long as you are eating, drinking and finding your way safely on your own.

Thank God for loving you enough to allow you to know Him. Thank Him for sending Jesus. Through Jesus' sacrificial death on the cross our debts were forgiven (no matter how large or small). Apart from Christ, we could never experience God's love, compassion, redemption and strength.

Meet God in His Word

Humility is simply agreeing with God about two things:

1. _____

2. _____

Reread Luke 7:40-48. What comparison was Jesus making between the woman and the Pharisees in the room?

Why did the larger debtor love his moneylender more for canceling his debt?

What impacts your love for Jesus?

Face to Face with Jesus

Have you ever watched a baby's face when his mother or father stepped into the room? He could have been crying, playing or watching whatever was going on—then Mama or Daddy entered the room and his face illuminated with recognition, immediately he wanted to be held, he kicked his little feet and smiled. Mikel, my oldest daughter used to stretch her baby legs as far as they could reach, flex her toes, clench her fists and shake her head as she gurgled and cooed! Mikel, and other babies like her, respond with these expressions of pure adoration because they already return the love of their parents and they know they are special to them.

Would you perhaps take some time to love on God that way today? Would you recognize His great love toward you, acknowledge the precious personal relationship He allows you and get all excited about His presence in your life? If so, spend some time right now soaking in the revelations He's provided you this week. Reflect on who He says you are. Reflect on who He says He is. And thank Him for expressing His love to you. Choose one verse to print as a statement of praise:

MY PRAYER FOR TODAY

DAY 5
HUMBLE YOURSELF THEREFORE UNDER THE MIGHTY HAND OF GOD

Read John 12:1-11

Humility's Power

Humility will bring you understanding which will lead to wisdom. Wisdom releases strength, power and the miraculous activity of God.

> *Humble yourself therefore under the mighty hand of God that He may exalt you at the proper time.*
>
> 2 Peter 5:6

Satan tries to deceive you and He uses pride to trap you. Take authority over your enemy by reminding him that you agree with God about who you are...and you agree with God about who He is.

There are some ways of measuring your humility quotient. Read these statements carefully and print PRIDE in each space:

If I am complaining..._____ is stealing my joy.

If I am overwhelmed..._____ has stolen my peace.

If I am worried..._____ is choking my faith.

If I am depressed..._____ has blinded me to who God says I am.

If I am discouraged..._____ has deafened me to whom God says He is.

Too often we allow anxiety, pressure, discouragement and depression to move in with our life's circumstances. We fear we are at their mercy until our circumstances change. We jokingly refer to our defeat by saying we're living in the "to" part of *"from glory to ever-increasing glory."*

But this is not so! Anxiety, stress, discouragement and depression...these are signs that PRIDE is choking humility in our hearts. Satan uses the same "life experiences" God allows to set traps for us. You can overwhelmingly conquer him and his ugly, defeating powers by carefully, thoroughly replacing PRIDE with humility.

Life's circumstances are not your enemy. Satan is. But when you embrace God's way of humility, you move effortlessly through life's circumstances and land in the arms of your loving Savior.

Meet God in His Word
Read John 12:9-11 again. The crowd came not only to see Jesus but Lazarus also. What did the chief priests plan to do about Lazarus?

How did their pride play into that plan?

Face to Face with Jesus
When you choose humility, you will replace:

• Complaints with **Gratitude. Gratitude is the vocal expression of humility.** (Philippians 4:6-7 remind us to be anxious for nothing but in all things to pray with THANKSGIVING...and the peace of God which transcends all understanding will guard your hearts and your minds in Christ Jesus.)

• Anxiety with **peace and joy. Peace and Joy are the internal results of humility.** (Nehemiah 8:10 says the joy of the Lord is your strength!)

• Defeat with **victory. Victory even in the midst of difficult circumstances is the reflection of Christ in you the hope of glory!** (Colossians 1:27)

This is very simple; we only have to do two things: Agree with God...

1. _____

2. _____

Thank God for the example of humility and pure expression of love this woman gave when she anointed Jesus with oil. Ask God to show you how you can pour your love on Him today.

MY PRAYER FOR TODAY

From the Heart of the Woman
Who Anointed Jesus
(A story based on Luke 7:36-50)

My father died suddenly while he was working. I'll never forget the men carrying his body to our house. My mother screamed and tore her clothes. She wailed throughout the night. Her weeping and his cold stiff body scared me. My mother never smiled again. After we buried Papa, Olivia (my two-year-old sister) tugged on my arm and cried. We were both hungry. We hadn't eaten for three days. We were poor before Papa died; I guess we were destitute now. I tried to get Mama's attention, but she just stared into space and rubbed Papa's belt between her fingers.

I took Olivia with me and left to find food. We had no money. I don't think I really knew what I'd do; only that Olivia needed to eat. When we got to the market, Olivia reached for an orange. I was thinking of how I could possibly offer to sweep or help set out fruit in exchange for food. I didn't see Olivia reach for the fruit; I only heard her cry in pain as the big heavy lady yelled, "You wretched urchin! Don't even think about stealing from me!" She swatted Olivia's hand with a strip whip made from camel's hair.

Olivia's eyes filled with tears; her chubby little hand swelled where the woman slapped her. I lost all control; the grief, fear and hopelessness of the past few days engulfed me and I lunged at the lady. "You wicked witch!" I screamed. She fell back, heavy on the baskets of potatoes, and I scrambled to get Olivia in one arm while I grabbed two oranges with the other. We ran blindly as people began to gather behind us. When we were safe, Olivia and I sat down to eat our oranges. Terror, pain and guilt filled my stomach so that I couldn't eat the fruit. Instead I watched Olivia devour hers—juice dripping from her chin.

That day marked the beginning of our fight for survival. Mama never came out of her suffering. Within the year we buried her too. No one knew what to say. I was 15 and plenty old enough to be married, but Mama and Papa hadn't planned that far ahead, so Olivia and I were all alone.

I'd learned to steal more discretely. Olivia was a beautiful child with a sweet disposition. She would pretend to be lost; I taught her to sniff an onion so that her eyes watered. And while she cried great big crocodile tears, I filled a bag with food, hid it under my robe, then with great flare I'd scoop her up, scolding her for getting away from Mama.

I met Darius almost by accident. He bumped me, or maybe I bumped him, on the way out of the marketplace and I dropped a few figs. Eyeing me suspiciously, he smiled, "How about you meet me at dusk by the old stone wall at the edge of town, and I'll pretend I didn't see that." Because he was a Roman soldier, what choice did I have? I told Olivia to stay in the house, and with all the courage I could muster, I walked to the old stone wall just down the path from our home. I knew it well. No one would see anything that might happen. Even if they did see, they wouldn't get involved in the illicit affairs of a Roman soldier for fear of their own life! And although I was afraid, my drive for survival overruled my fear, and bravely I kept my promise to meet him.

Surprisingly Darius was kind. I actually enjoyed his attention. But because we couldn't be properly married, He just came and went as he pleased. Our neighbors began to talk. I begged Darius to stay with us always, to be my husband. But he just laughed and said, "Why mess up a good thing?" With that he'd plant a kiss on my forehead and be on his way.

I didn't know how the Roman's assigned their soldiers to specific duties, so I took Darius' word when he explained that he had to leave for a few months. Olivia and I both missed him terribly. When he returned, he rushed into our home waving a sealed document. To my surprise, Darius presented me with divorce papers. He explained that his father arranged his marriage to Elsa, and that he never really loved her like he loved me. Darius left out the part about his and Elsa's two children.

At first I was stunned. If Darius were married all that time, then I'd committed adultery, but seeing my troubled expression, Darius quickly twirled me around and said we could now be married! Immediately we went to the Roman court and married. Now Olivia and I had a respectable home. We could be real citizens of our community. Of course my Jewish neighbors no longer talked to us. We were dead to them because we not only consorted with the Gentiles, but I'd chosen to marry a divorced Roman soldier! For a few months Darius poured his adoration on us. I held my head high as I marched through the marketplace purchasing food—lots of food—in an attempt to make up for years of poverty!

I was proud of my swelling belly and the baby Darius was giving me. I wanted those self-righteous Jews to know I was just fine without their God and all His infinite rules! But then, the dream began to fade. At first Darius was distant and quiet. Then he'd stay out late and come home inebriated. I feared he regretted his decision to leave his first wife for me. All the pleading, begging and crying did nothing but seal my fate. Before the baby was even born, Darius was gone. I received an official notice of divorce from the Roman court a few weeks later.

I was not yet 20 years old, single and pregnant. I was a thief and an adulterer. I'd married a Roman—a despised Gentile—and been rejected by the same. What could I do? Where could I go? I'd never been particularly religious before. Papa read from the Torah and we ate the traditional Passover supper, but that was the extent of our "religion." The God I'd heard about didn't seem worth my effort. He was full of rules and unattainable moral standards. Though no one ever actually said so, I just knew I couldn't measure up.

But now, should I try? Should I go to the Pharisees, confess all my sins and get right with God before I brought a baby into the world?

I looked at Olivia's soft innocent eyes and thought of my own guilt. I'd even pulled her down with me! I brushed the dust off Papa's Torah and started reading. I was shocked at what I found. This God was more serious about sin than I'd known! The punishment for theft...cut off the hand; the punishment for adultery...stoning! I couldn't go to the Pharisees. They might kill me for Jehovah's sake! My fate was sealed. I'd done too many things wrong. I'd just have to teach Olivia and my baby that, in this cruel life, you have to look out for yourself.

One day I heard some of the men talking excitedly about a strange man who preached in the desert. They said he urged sinners to repent and be baptized! They said he was making quite a stir among the Pharisees. He told people the only way to God was through repentance and the forgiveness of sin.

God wanted to forgive sin? The God I read about condemned and punished sin! Could this same God forgive?

I was curious. I told Olivia we were going on a trip. We packed our bags and took off to the Jordan River where we heard John preach. He was the strangest man I'd ever seen! His hair stuck out in all directions. He was dirty and thin. He yelled when he spoke, "Repent! For the kingdom of heaven is here!"

People all around me were crying. Some of them were banging their heads on the ground in grief. The growing baby in my womb felt like an iron ball of shame and regret. What was I to do?

"Repent! Be baptized!" John screeched.

Then he started talking to the tax collectors, "Be fair! Collect only what you ought to collect!" And to the wealthy men he pointed and said, "Share what you have with those who have nothing!"

I thought of the fat lady who obviously had more than enough and how she'd smacked Olivia's hand. I wished she were here! But then, that strange prophet seemed to look at me and he shouted, "No one will escape the wrath of God! Repent!"

My knees buckled beneath me, and I started to move forward and follow those who were being baptized. That was when I saw Him. He was all alone. He looked like he had a very important mission to accomplish. He walked with dignity and authority. Where everyone else was slumped over in grief and regret, this man walked with majesty and an aura of, what could it be...holiness. That's it. He walked with his head lifted high and not even a hint of shame in His expression.

John saw Him too. He pointed to Jesus and said, "I baptize you with water. But one more powerful than me is coming! I am not even worthy to tie His sandals. He will baptize you with the Holy Spirit and fire."

That was an unusual thing to say! I was confused. But, I couldn't take my eyes off this man. John turned to face us and said, "This is the lamb of God. He will take away the sins of the world."

The Lamb of God. You mean, like the Passover lamb? This man could take away my sin? Is it possible God can forgive sin? Is it possible God *wants* to forgive sin?

I watched Jesus insist John baptize Him. We stood in silence as Jesus was baptized, and a quiet murmur flowed through the crowd when a dove came down from heaven and rested on Jesus' shoulder. I strained to catch a glimpse of His face. Who was this mysterious "lamb of God"?

Jesus left the crowd without looking back. I can't really describe how I felt. I don't know about the others, but suddenly I had a spark of hope in my sin-filled heart. I waited my turn to be baptized, and when the rough hands of John wrapped around my wrists, I prayed for the first time in my life, "Oh God, if You are a forgiving God, please forgive me. I am so full of sin!"

Olivia and I returned home. We never stole again. I set up a respectable business as a seamstress. We weren't rich, but we could now eat and clothe ourselves without stealing. The only luxury I purchased was an alabaster jar of expensive perfume. Call me sentimental, but it was a gift I purchased for my girls when I finally made enough money in honest work. I wanted Olivia and sweet Aremis to know they were valued, and to feel beautiful even if we had to work hard for every bite we ate. I also wanted to celebrate the fact that I could rise above my life of crime. The perfume was a symbol of my self-sufficiency and my tenacity. I was saving it for just the right time; perhaps Olivia's wedding or Aremis' 12th birthday. But for now the alabaster jar was placed where the three of us could see it every day; and when we saw it there, we knew that we *could*, we *would*, survive this life no matter what!

Through the years, the flicker of hope that started burning in my heart at the Jordan River calmed to a glowing ember. I hadn't given much more thought to my need for forgiveness. I had, after all established myself as a somewhat respectable business woman. And, although the Jews and Gentiles alike did business with me, I no longer cared that the Jews would forever consider me a "sinner."

However, late at night when my girls were sleeping, I'd lie awake and wonder if there was hope for me. Could I really be made clean? Sure John and the Jordan River washed me that day, but there had to be more.

I'd just delivered Mary's robe the week before, and I knew Lazarus was sick but Mary assured me Jesus would come and make him well. Jesus often stayed in their home on His way to and from Jerusalem. I don't know why I'd never taken time to gather with others outside the windows while He was there. Many curious people did so. I often heard them tell about how He healed someone. Or they'd have heated arguments over what He meant when He talked about the kingdom of heaven. I guess Lazarus' death came as a surprise to all of us. Jesus never came! Lazarus was sick several days, and the servant delivered the message. But Jesus didn't come! My curiosity drove me to press past the Jews, who wished I hadn't come, and join the mourners at their home that day. We wailed as we gave our best effort toward properly mourning the death of such a kind man.

Suddenly, Jesus was among us. I overheard Him talking to Martha. After greeting Mary, He told us to be quiet and gave instructions for them to remove the stone at the entrance of Lazarus' tomb. Martha objected! In all practicality, she urged Jesus not to do such a thing. His body had been in the tomb for four days, and there would be a strong smell. The smell of death is overwhelming! But Jesus insisted, so they rolled the stone away. He prayed aloud; then with a great powerful voice He said, "Lazarus, come forth!"

You would have had to be there to get the full impact of Lazarus' resurrection from the dead. Our sorrow turned into rejoicing. Some of the mourners shouted; some fainted; I just watched. Jesus turned His head our way and made eye contact with me. Time stood still. What was it He'd said to Martha: "I am the resurrection and the life. He who believes in me will live." At that moment I knew; Jesus is the Lamb of God. God does love sinners. He wants to forgive us. God loves me. He wants to forgive my sin. My guilt and regret melted away. That ember of hope burst into a roaring flame and filled my heart with laughter. I ran home and shared my newfound hope with Olivia. I held Aremis in my arms and rejoiced in God's goodness toward me. The God whose laws were so strict loved me with unending love. He forgives!

The time of the Passover was coming. We'd never celebrated before, but this year would be different. Now I knew Jehovah loved me, and I wanted Olivia and Aremis to know this too. As Olivia and I prepared the dinner, John's words rang in my head: "Behold, the Lamb of God." The Passover lamb was offered for Israel's sin. The lamb symbolically took the sin of the people upon himself and was then slain to atone for that sin. Jehovah received the sacrificial lamb as an offering. His wrath could be placed there, and the people could be spared.

Jesus is the Lamb of God.

I was looking over the lambs that were brought in for the Passover feasts, searching for the one for us when it dawned on me.

"Behold, the lamb!"

What if Jesus were to take our sin on Himself and be slain like that lamb? Jesus would die! That gentle, kind, good man was willing to die for me! Before it was too late, I had to let Him know how much I loved Him. I had to let Him know how grateful I was for His forgiveness. I had to let Him know He changed my life! I had to let Him know He'd given me life! Where I'd only existed before, Jesus opened my heart and my mind to hope and a great future. I had to let Jesus know.

Olivia held Aremis as I carefully wrapped the alabaster box in a cloth. I explained to Olivia that this perfume would be perfect to express my gratitude to Jesus. I tried to share with her my urgency. She didn't understand. How could she? We'd never even celebrated the Passover before! She didn't understand the lamb of God. We discovered He was at the home of a Pharisee named Simon. I shuttered to think that I'd have to interrupt His meal at a Pharisee's house, but I was so determined to give this gift to Jesus before it was too late, that I didn't even care.

There was no time for permission and protocol. No Pharisee in his right mind would welcome me into his home anyway. Olivia and Aremis waited at the door. I saw Jesus reclining by the table. I walked right over to Him, even as He talked. When I bowed at His feet, the tears started flowing; sweet, gentle tears. They were slow and steady. I cried because He loved me. I cried because He cared. I cried because I knew that even though I'd broken most every rule God had ever written, there was forgiveness in His heart. I cried because He was the lamb of God. I cried because I knew, deep in my soul, that He was going to pay the penalty for my sin. I cried because I knew He would pay the penalty for even those who would never know. I poured the perfume on His beautiful, weathered and weary feet. The rich fragrance filled the room. For just a moment everyone was silent.

It was a holy hush.

Then, a Pharisee muttered beneath his breath, "Humph. If this man were really a prophet, he would know what kind of woman this is that is doing this to him. He would know she is a sinner." Others murmured, "What a waste! This perfume could have been sold and the money given to the poor!" Jesus addressed these comments much to their chagrin. I'm sure they didn't intend for Jesus to hear them.

Jesus put His gentle hand on the back of my head, and peace flooded my soul.

"Leave her alone; she has done a beautiful thing to me." He continued to address the Pharisee, "Simon, do you see this woman? I came into your house. You didn't give me water for my feet, but she wet my feet with her tears and wiped them with her hair. You did not give me a kiss, but this woman, from the time I entered, has not stopped kissing my feet. You didn't put oil on my head, but she has poured perfume on my feet. Therefore, I tell you, her many sins have been forgiven—for she loved much. But he who has been forgiven little loves little."

He addressed His indignant disciples, "The poor you will always have with you, and you can help them anytime you want. But you will not always have

Me. She did what she could. She poured perfume on My body beforehand to prepare for My burial."

Then He lifted my chin to look in my eyes. His attention penetrated past my tears to the hidden depths of my heart. Gently He said, "Your sins are forgiven."

All of them. The lady I shoved...forgiven. The oranges I stole...forgiven. The tricks I led Olivia to play...forgiven. Darius...forgiven. All of them, forgiven.

"Your faith has saved you; go in peace."

Behold, the Lamb of God. He takes away the sins of the world.

Questions for Reflection

1. Share a time you felt rejected.

2. Why do so few people genuinely express their love and concern for others?

3. What is humility?

4. How does God feel about pride? Why?

5. How did it make you feel to read the verses that tell you who God says you are? Which verse meant the most to you?

6. Share how God has proven Himself to be who He says He is in your life.

7. Which of the pride indicators do you struggle with in your life?

8. How did the woman who anointed Jesus demonstrate humility?

9. How can you demonstrate humility as you express your love to Jesus this week?

Ask God To

- Show you where pride is choking humility in your heart.
- Give you an opportunity to demonstrate humility this week.
- Give you the name of someone who will benefit from your genuine expression of love and concern in his or her life.

MY PRAYER FOR THIS WEEK

A VERSE TO MEMORIZE

*Without faith it is impossible to please God
because anyone who comes to Him must believe
that He exists and that He rewards
those who earnestly seek Him.*

—

Hebrews 11:6

CHAPTER 4

A Sick Woman and a Dead Girl

WOMAN TOUCHED BY JESUS
The Woman Who Was Healed by Touching Jesus' Robe
Mark 5:21-43

INTRODUCTION
"A Sick Woman and a Dead Girl"

My Bible has this straightforward title above the story of the woman who was healed from her issue of blood when Jesus was on His way to a Pharisee's home to heal a little girl. The two people we'll study are the woman who was healed and Jairus (the Pharisee).

First let's consider the woman. When I was being treated for infertility, I had to subject my body to poking and prodding that went far past any modicum of modesty. I wonder if the woman Jesus healed of her issue of blood felt like I did that day the doctor discussed my "situation" as if it were merely medical research, as he demonstrated how to carefully gather endometrial tissue for the lab. The Bible tells us she endured *much* at the hands of *many* physicians. But after exhausting her resources, she still had her problem and it was worse than before. I have to wonder how a woman who'd experienced years of defeat could have so much faith in Jesus! She believed that if she could just touch the hem of His robe she would be healed. Jesus Himself was impressed with her faith.

Then, there was Jairus, a ruler of the synagogue. He demonstrated humility as he fell at Jesus' feet and "pleaded" with Him to come to his house and heal his twelve-year-old daughter. Jairus obviously believed in the miraculous power of Jesus, and his great need removed any preoccupation with theological arguments. Jairus' daughter was dying, and he believed Jesus could make her well.

As we look at the faith of these two desperate people, we'll learn that faith releases the power of God.

DAY 1
TWO FAITHS, ONE JESUS

Read Mark 5:21-36

Pray in Faith Believing

One summer afternoon, Kaleigh and TJ were playing together in the pool. I heard Kaleigh ask TJ to share his pool toys. He had the ball and the torpedo. Kaleigh said, "TJ, you've got both toys and that's not fair. I should have at least one."

To which TJ diplomatically replied, "Which one do you want?"

Kaleigh quickly responded, "The torpedo."

I looked up from my yard work to see if somehow my children had miraculously worked through this conflict. Sure enough, TJ shared the toys—only he gave Kaleigh the ball rather than the torpedo. I proceeded to chastise him, "TJ, why did you give Kaleigh the ball when she asked for the torpedo?"

But TJ didn't answer; Kaleigh did. "Oh, Mama, I knew he'd do that—so I asked for the one I didn't want, knowing he'd give me the one I really wanted!"

> *Without faith it is impossible to please God because anyone who comes to Him must believe that He exists and that He rewards those who earnestly seek Him.*
> Hebrews 11:6

Kaleigh knew her brother's character so she asked accordingly. Sometimes we approach God like Kaleigh approached TJ. We pray, "Oh God, please...oh if You just would...help Matilda to feel some sort of comfort while she wastes away in that hospital!" When what we really want is this, "Lord, heal Matilda—be glorified in her life!" We don't ask for what we really want because our faith is small, and we misjudge the character of God.

Kaleigh was right in the way she handled her brother, for TJ's character is obviously full of brotherly sin. However, God's character is full of perfect love! He is pleased when we trust Him, and when we come to Him fully aware of His desire to do for us what is best. God is looking for us to ask Him to do what He already wants to do on our behalf! He yearns for His people to seek

His face (turn from their wicked ways), honor Him, and expect Him to pour blessings out like a floodgate from heaven.

Meet God in His Word
Compare Jairus' faith with that of the woman:

Did your comparison include the fact that Jarius *pleaded* with Jesus out of desperate fear? Notice that Jarius also told Jesus what He must do in order to make His daughter well. Fill in the Blanks:

Please _____ and put your _____ on her so that she will be healed and live. (Mark 5:23)

How does this compare to the woman? What thought went through her mind? Fill in the Blanks:

"If I could just _____ His _____, I _____ be healed. (Mark 5:28)

While Jairus directed his attention to his great need, the woman directed her attention to Jesus' great power.

Face to Face with Jesus
Faith chooses to focus on God rather than the problem. Faith chooses to look past the mountain of impossibility to the Lord of the impossible. Have you got a big problem? Don't forget you've got a bigger God! Spend some time

today agreeing with David that God is bigger than any mountain you might face. Read Psalm 24.

Who is this King of glory? The Lord almighty—He is the King of glory.

MY PRAYER FOR TODAY

DAY 2
PHARISAICAL FOG

Read Mark 5:21-24

Pharisaical Fog

Jairus actually overcame great barriers to come to Jesus, fall at His feet and plead with Him. As a ruler of the synagogue, Jairus had to be surrounded by men who considered Jesus their enemy. His friends and colleagues engaged in constant verbal banter with Jesus seeking to catch Him in some religious discrepancy. However, Jairus' little girl was going to die, and his love for his daughter far outweighed his prestigious position. Therefore, Jairus sought Jesus in his hour of desperate need.

Have you ever wondered why the religious leaders had such a hard time believing in Jesus? They were amazed at His teaching and challenged by His wisdom, but they failed to recognize Him as the Son of God. Supposedly they were the ones who knew the most *about* God. They spoke *for* God. They appointed themselves *keepers* of God's law, and they *represented* God. But somewhere along the way their spiritual vision was blurred.

> *Without faith it is impossible to please God because anyone who comes to Him must believe that He exists and that He rewards those who earnestly seek Him.*
> Hebrews 11:6

The blur came when they distorted the love of God by elevating the law above love. With pride they determined how man could work his way to near perfection and suggested that, when every "i" was dotted and every "t" crossed, truly serious students of the law could stand proudly before a righteous, holy God. Their steps to success were so complicated that, when they climbed the difficult heights, they felt justified in waving their accomplishments like a banner over the heads of mere men and honored one another with high and lofty position in their world.

Jesus presented several problems for them. *If* the common man could establish a right relationship with God through a simple invitation—"Jesus, please forgive me from my sins, save me so I can go to heaven with You when I die"—then how could the years of sacrifice and discipline be rewarded? How could the religious leaders be highly esteemed if their hard work was not necessary?

Another problem Jesus presented the Pharisees was that of claiming to have authority to forgive sin. This was the single most significant tool the Pharisees had for ruling over other Jews. Through their study and interpretation of Scripture, they could determine which person could be restored to the fellowship of the community, and which could not. Many times their decisions were based on selfish ulterior motives. Who gave Jesus authority to forgive sin? What did He mean coming to earth and claiming even greater authority than they possessed?

In all four gospels (Matthew, Mark, Luke and John) as much attention is given to Jesus' confrontations with the Pharisees as is given to His miraculous ministry. I wondered about that. What does God have for us to learn from the Pharisees? Are we in danger today of becoming like them? How can we guard ourselves against the pharisaical fog that blurs our spiritual vision?

Meet God in His Word

God reveals Himself to the "pure in heart." Read Matthew 18:1-4. Print verse 4 in the space provided:

According to this verse, whom will God welcome into His kingdom?

The day my nephew was buried, we gathered at Tom's parents' home. The wind was blowing gently on that beautiful autumn day. My three children (Mikel, 11, Kaleigh, 10 and TJ, 8) joined their cousins (ages 11, 10 and 7). None of them were sure about what all was going on, and most of them were participating in their first funeral experience. They were understandably quiet and subdued when we first arrived. But after a few minutes in the grief filled house, they decided to go outside on the front porch.

I glanced out the window and saw a picture of absolute trust and childlike innocence. All the cousins were laughing out loud as they ran through the blowing leaves and twirled around completely filled with delight in this October shower of God's glory. Even in the midst of their indescribable loss, they were confident that God had everything under control—and He showered His presence over our hearts with the picture of their confidence in Him. Even when they soiled their dress up clothes with leaf juice and tree sap as the dance gave way to climbing a few trees, we didn't care, for God was speaking comfort to us through our children.

Many of the Pharisees forgot what God knows all too well. Read Psalm 103:14 and fill in the blanks:

For He knows how we are formed, He remembers that we are _____

_____.

The Pharisees forgot they were merely dust. They relished the authority they had over the people and cherished the power and honor they received. They began to think of themselves as gods to their people. They took full advantage of every opportunity to separate themselves from the common man and reign over them with piety and ridiculous expansion of God's original laws.

We wouldn't do that today, would we? I pray not.

But in some parts of denominational work, and in some churches I've visited, I've witnessed a lifting up of the leaders to such a degree that the leaders being lifted up begin to believe the great things said about them. They live lavish lifestyles and expect homage and respect from those they lead. In some places I've been, more attention is given to proper procedure toward pomp and circumstance than is given to prayer. I've met some leaders who would not dare admit that they desperately need God to work in and through them. I've been among staff who would not dream of letting their congregations know how insignificant and weak they truly are. I was even told once to be careful not to let those "out there" (in the churches I served) know that I didn't have all the answers.

This attitude teeters on the beginnings of pharisaical fog. I can't lead that way! I can't live that way. My friends, *I don't have all the answers!* I desperately need God to work in and through me; there's no other way to thrive in His kingdom!

Face to Face with Jesus

Don't give in to the temptation to consider yourself more important than you ought. Read Philippians 2:1-13. Ask God to impress on you the importance of coming to Him as a child. Be reminded that "it is God who works in you both to will and to act according to His good purpose."

MY PRAYER FOR TODAY

DAY 3
"FAITH IS BEING SURE OF WHAT WE HOPE FOR AND CERTAIN OF WHAT WE DO NOT SEE."

Read Mark 5:24-29

Faith Is Seeing What Does Not Exist As If It Were Real

Nineteen years ago Tom and I were counting the days until his final term at Southwestern Seminary came to completion. I graduated in May. Tom was to graduate in December. We couldn't wait to complete our formal education and go wherever God was preparing for us to serve.

Those were exciting days. We received phone calls and letters from churches all over the United States. We tediously completed questionnaires and surveys sent to us by pastor search committees. We flipped the pages of our Rand McNally road atlas and searched for obscure locations like Tombstone, Arizona. We sent résumés and prayers to Maryland, Alabama, Texas, Arizona, Florida, Georgia and Tennessee. We knelt beside our bed and prayed, asking God to show us His direction and give us His place of ministry.

> *Without faith it is impossible to please God because anyone who comes to Him must believe that He exists and that He rewards those who earnestly seek Him.*
>
> Hebrews 11:6

When Earl Waldrop called, we went to our atlas and searched for a small community called Thompson Station, 30 miles south of Nashville, Tennessee. There it was, designated by the tiniest dot on highway 31 between Franklin and Columbia. We agreed to meet Earl and Jo (his wife) and take a tour of the community while we were visiting with Tom's family over the Christmas holidays.

During that tour we saw some of the most beautiful landscape you could imagine. Middle Tennessee is blanketed in rolling hills and sprinkled with trees. I could see our children living in a gentle quiet place like this. But, there seemed to be more cows than people. There was one neighborhood with about 30 homes that had been built some 15 or 20 years before. Everyone else lived at the end of long gravel driveways surrounded by livestock. I voiced my concern, "Jo, why are you all planting a church here? There don't seem to be very many people and there's already a church three miles down the road." Jo immediately shared her faith: "We believe this community is going to grow. And a growing community needs a new church, one that will reach out to the new people moving in." While I saw pastures, Jo saw future growth.

A month later we were serving as the first full-time pastor and wife of the Thompson Station Baptist Mission. There were eight to twelve active members of our fellowship. On Tom's first Sunday as pastor, he said, "We will have over 100 in this place next year at this time." God allowed Tom to see what was not.

The next week all eight of our committed members called us to give us counsel. "Brother Tom, we appreciate your enthusiasm, but we've been here ten years and we have yet to have fifty people in our congregation! We just don't want you to set your hopes too high only to be discouraged." Those phone calls were intended to calm us down, to speak reality into our newly graduated hearts. But they had the opposite effect. For every call we received urging us to lower our expectations, we began to see one more family that didn't have a church home. Maybe Jo's growth was coming, but we weren't going to wait for it. Prior to any new neighborhoods in our community, we saw a church running 100, 200, maybe even 300 in attendance. God allowed us to see Thompson Station the way He was seeing this rural community.

Tom hung a map in his home office. He marked houses with a red marker. Then, he placed straight pins in the map to indicate the homes he visited. Most every night of the week, Tom knocked on doors in our community. Saturdays would come and we'd both venture out knocking on doors. Our invitation was simple, "Hi, I'm Tom, this is my wife Leighann and I'm the new pastor at the Baptist church meeting in the converted honky tonk across from the railroad tracks. We'd love to have you worship with us if you don't have a church home."

Some came, some didn't. But a year later on our anniversary Sunday we had 113 in worship. "Faith is being sure of what we hope for and certain of what we do not see."

Faith compels us to put forth effort. Faith tells us that our work is not in vain! The first door Tom and I knocked on together was slammed in our face. The woman we met told us that she was perfectly happy worshipping alone in her heart, and that if she wanted to attend church she could certainly do so without a personal invitation from us. I'd love to tell you that I walked away praying for her and whatever bitterness made her so ill. But instead, I walked away thinking only of myself. I'd moved here in high hopes of serving the people and growing a great church, only to be greeted by the first person with anger and hostility. I *felt* like going home and calling Tombstone, Arizona, to tell them Tom and I would be glad to consider coming to pastor their retirement community church. But faith led us to the next house on the street. Tom still saw God's church in Thompson Station. At the next house we were greeted warmly. Only a few weeks later we sat in that kitchen and led David to Jesus. As soon as the weather got warm enough we baptized him in a backyard swimming pool. Throughout the first year, God added seven more families from that neighborhood to the two that were already attending our church. Our first young adult Sunday School class was birthed when those neighbors decided to get involved in our little church. Every small group we have today started from that one.

Today we have 90 Sunday School classes (we call them Connect Groups now) with over 1,500 in attendance. Our worship attendance is approaching 2,000 and growing steadily. Jesus said in Matthew 17:20 that if you have faith as small as a mustard seed you can say to the mountain, "Move from here to there" and it will move. He assures us that "nothing is impossible for you."

Tom and I believed God for over 100 on our first anniversary Sunday. And God gave us 113. We adjusted our faith and believed Him for 200, 300, 500 and so on. Every time we believed we had to knock on doors, create new units for small groups, increase our budget and build buildings. Each time our faith was stretched. We didn't have money, we didn't have teachers, and we didn't have land. But because we believed, God provided. As we walk in faith, He does for us what we cannot do for ourselves.

God has certainly proven Himself faithful to us. But we won't stop here. Jo Waldrop was right. This community is now one of the fastest growing communities in the nation. And for every person attending our church, there are hundreds who still need to be impacted by the incredible love and power of God.

Meet God in His Word

So, what is faith, and how can we develop our faith? Hebrews 11:1 says, "Now faith is being sure of what we hope for and certain of what we do not see."

Where is God challenging you to believe Him? Is it in a loved one's heart and life? Is it in your business, your home or your ministry?

What has He shown you that does not yet exist? Will you believe? Will you work as if God's promise is true? Tell Him so right now.

Face to Face with Jesus:

Invite God to increase your faith so that you can live your life pleasing to Him.

MY PRAYER FOR TODAY

DAY 4
A WORD ABOUT SUFFERING

Read Mark 5:21-26

Why Do We Suffer So?

This is what I wrote the day after my nephew was buried:

Ryan was twenty years old, tragically, senselessly killed in a car accident. His accident cost the lives of two other young men as well. He was the only son of Tom's brother David. David lost his wife a year ago after a long illness and painful death to a rare lung disease. When Tom and I got word that Ryan was killed, we were returning home from a weekend prayer conference and happened to be near the Dickson, Tennessee, exit on interstate 40. We decided to swing by David's house and visit with him. When we walked into his home I immediately sensed an enormous burden of suffering.

How can we even begin to make sense of this? Yesterday as Tom lead the funeral service, the picture of Jesus weeping at Lazarus' funeral came to my mind. I found comfort in realizing that Jesus weeps with us when we experience death's sting. Some of the women at Ryan's funeral were beyond weeping; they were wailing. Though this was uncomfortable to me, I considered how healthy that might be to go ahead and allow the emotional turmoil to give release and cry out in desperation. So many of the people gathered there did not have a personal, intimate relationship with God and, therefore, did not know the strength His Holy Spirit provides in life's darkest hour. As the Holy Spirit ministered to me, and as evidence of His ministry poured out of the tear-stained eyes of my children, I prayed for those who didn't know Him.

> Without faith it is impossible to please God because anyone who comes to Him must believe that He exists and that He rewards those who earnestly seek Him.
>
> Hebrews 11:6

Why do we suffer so? Perhaps we ask the wrong questions. Suffering is a fact of life. Why, I do not know. Don and Sterline are Tom's parents. Only eight and a half years ago we buried one of their sons, Tom's brother James. He was killed a day before his 38th birthday in a motorcycle accident. He left behind a wife and two daughters (then ages 14 and 2). Only a few months ago Sterline's brother Jim buried his wife after a long battle with cancer. Jim also lost a child several years ago when she hemorrhaged in her brain while sleeping.

Suffering is a fact of life. The Pharisees tried to explain it, but Jesus came to put the record straight and assured us that trying to explain suffering is futile. Jesus didn't come to alleviate our suffering. He didn't even come to take away our pain. We have missed the point if we expect Him to do so. Jesus came to give us hope—hope that reaches beyond death's door to life everlasting.

Meet God in His Word

When we read the story of the sick woman and the dead girl, we can't miss the fact of the woman's suffering. How long had this woman been subject to her bleeding?

How much suffering had she endured? What did her suffering cost her?

And after all this suffering, what did she receive? Instead of getting better she grew _____.

Why do people have to suffer?

Read Matthew 5:43-45. In verse 44, whom does Jesus say to love and pray for?

Did Jesus assume enemies and persecution would be part of the Christian life?

Who does God cause the sun to rise on? Who does God cause the rain to fall on?

Is suffering only and always a natural result of sin?

Is suffering ever the natural result of sin?

Can suffering impact every life?

Face to Face with Jesus

Is it our responsibility to make sense of suffering to the unbelievers around us?

No! Never! Our job is not to explain suffering to those who are suffering. According to these verses, Jesus' instructions to us are to love people. The best way for us to respond to grief when God allows suffering to strike deep in the hearts of those who do not know Him, is to wrap God's loving arms physically around their broken hearts and speak words of love.

I'm going to be real honest with you. Tom and I had to make ourselves take that detour by David's house. We didn't know what to say. We didn't know what to do. We were trying desperately to absorb the tragic fact of the loss in our own hearts and minds. When we arrived, we simply hugged him and told him we loved him. Several times David said, "There's really nothing anyone can say." To which we responded, "Yeah." We sat in silence and shared his darkness.

When I saw Ryan's mother at the funeral, I simply hugged her neck and said, "We share your grief; we are crying with you." That's all, nothing more! Jesus wept. So should we.

Has suffering hit your family? Have you been tempted to ask the wrong questions? Would you be willing to simply agree that suffering is unfortunately a fact of life? Ask God to be the God of all comfort to you and to those He allows you to comfort. Read 2 Corinthians 1:3-7.

MY PRAYER FOR TODAY

DAY 5
THERE ARE NO INTERRUPTIONS
IN JESUS' SCHEDULE

Read Mark 5:27-36

Busy-ness and Kingdom Effectiveness

Let me recap Tom's weekend for you. Friday we left for a prayer conference in Lexington, TN. Tom preached four times in two days. On our way home, Saturday afternoon we discovered Ryan had been killed in a car accident and we visited with David. Sunday morning Tom preached twice in our own church. That afternoon he went to Dickson to be with his family and to begin preparations for the funeral. He returned home after 10:00 Sunday night. Monday Tom performed the funeral and got back home late in the afternoon just in time to turn around and make the hour drive to Etheridge, TN to preach at a gathering of churches. In Etheridge, Tom was amazed at the crowd of people gathered for encouragement. Tom delivered his sermon and fulfilled the final ministry task of the long weekend.

> *Without faith it is impossible to please God because anyone who comes to Him must believe that He exists and that He rewards those who earnestly seek Him.*
>
> Hebrews 11:6

When David asked Tom to do Ryan's funeral, his face went white and we both trembled at the thought of such an assignment. How could he minister in the midst of his own grief? But, as David realized the weight of his request, he quickly acquiesced and said he could ask the local pastor to do it for them. Only, he didn't know that man's name and that pastor would not really know Ryan. Tom and I both knew this was God's ministry for him. Although he was very concerned about his ability to minister in such raw emotional upheaval, he had a solemn conviction that God would strengthen him for the task. I knew God would work powerfully in and through Tom.

Tom asked our church to pray for him. He met with Ryan's closest friends and family and gathered meaningful tidbits of information he could share to ease our pain. Tom collected Ryan's Bible and sought God's guidance. As he prepared, he knew God had a message for the crowd that would be gathered there; he gave his body for God to use to communicate it to us.

Because God is always faithful, and able to strengthen us beyond imagination, Tom completed the tasks of the weekend. He felt the power of God course through him Sunday, Sunday afternoon and evening. Monday afternoon he spoke boldly God's message of salvation at Ryan's funeral. And again Monday night Tom sensed the power of God literally holding him up as he exhorted the Christians in Etheridge to continue strong in the work of the ministry.

How did he do this? How did he manage such a weekend? Tom didn't; God did. God supernaturally provides power to obedient servants through the inner working of His Holy Spirit. Tom was exhausted last night, understandably so...but left early this morning to serve his role on the state convention's executive board.

Ryan's death was not an interruption in our hectic ministry lives; his death was the ministry God had for us this weekend.

Jesus was a busy man. He often found His best time to pray late at night, all night or early in the morning. The rest of His day was filled with people and their needs. Sometimes He tried to take His disciples away for much needed rest, only to have the crowds of needy people go ahead of Him and meet Him there.

Jesus came to earth with a divine mission. He came to build a bridge between us and God! Amazingly, Jesus' official ministry took place in three years! Think about that. Three years. Three years doesn't even get you a college degree. Three years comes and goes in the blink of an eye. When I turned 33 I thought about the fact that I was as old as Jesus when His mission on earth was complete! How did He do that?

Jesus *didn't* do a lot of things we think we *have* to do. And He was never bothered by interruptions. He walked with a sense of purpose. He was certain of His activity and sure of His future. Jesus spent a great deal of time praying and seeking instruction from His Father. When He started His ministry, He stayed 40 days in the wilderness preparing for what was to come. When He faced the cross, He spent His last few hours in the Garden of Gethsemane pouring His heart out to God in preparation for the suffering that was to come.

Meet God in His Word

Jesus provided us an example of how we ought to live our lives of ministry. Read John 14:8-10. Fill in the Blanks:

Rather, it is the _____ living in me, who is doing his

_____.

Who does the work of God?

Did you say, God? **God does the work of God.** We don't do the work of God. God does His own work *through* us! He is the potter; we are the clay. Because we've chosen to live our lives for Jesus, we no longer have authority over our day's schedule. We've given that to Him.

Jesus didn't have to know exactly how God was going to use Him that day. It was enough for Him to be in the place God wanted Him to be, then to be open to the activity God revealed to Him there. As the opportunities presented themselves, Jesus stepped forward to make the most of them! The woman healed in this week's story was in the crowd, and she pressed in to Him. Jesus didn't get up that morning wondering where He'd find her and how He'd finally heal her 12-year suffering. Jesus got up that morning and went to the other side of the lake.

Read Ephesians 5:15-17. Complete the following instructions.

Be very _____ then, how you live.

Make the _____ of every opportunity

Do not be _____

But _____ what the Lord's will is.

Face to Face with Jesus

Ever since I was 12 years old (that same age as Jairus' daughter when Jesus healed her), I wanted to know God's will for my life. Even today I struggle with whether I'm doing the right things and whether I'm pouring my energy in the right places. Jesus never wasted time wondering about these things. Following God is not about completing an assignment. God does not give us a "to do" list and expect us to mark it off as we go along.

Read your Bible—*check*

Pray—*check*

Write a note of encouragement—*check*

Call a friend—*check*

Witness to your neighbor—*check*

Pray with your children—*oops! I didn't do this today, oh no!*

No, God does not give us "to do" lists. This is more the method of the Pharisees. Jesus set an example for us in the way He approached His ministry. Get up in the morning, meet God privately, read His Word and pray. Ask Him to guide your steps today and watch for where He is working in the lives of people around you. If we ask Him, God will open our eyes and ears to His on-going activity in the lives of people we come in contact with.

"What about my vocation and activity?" you may ask. The answer is simple, keep doing what you're doing now until God tells you to do otherwise! God knows how to communicate His plans to you. God knows how to get His work done and how to place His workers where He needs them to work. He might make you restless, He may allow you to be downsized, He might give you a vision, or He may speak clearly to you in your quiet time. God may even promote you! He has a myriad of methods for moving you from where you are to where He may want you to be. In the meantime, rest in the fact that you are right where God wants you to be for right now, and watch for people He's personally assigned to you! Then, remember that you don't have to do anything but allow God free access to your heart, mind and mouth. Jesus explained to Philip, "the words I say are not just my own. Rather, it is the Father living in me, who is doing his work." He goes on to say, "I tell you the truth, anyone who has faith in me will do what I have been doing...He will do even greater things than these" (John 14:12).

What interruptions might God have for you today? Ask God to make you sensitive to the people around you. Ask Him to use you to pour His love on them today.

MY PRAYER FOR TODAY

From the Heart of the Woman Who Was Healed by Touching Jesus' Robe
(A story based on Mark 5:21-43)

When Papa told me of his plans to allow Eliud to marry me, I anticipated a future of marriage and family full of security and love, for that is all I'd known. Eliud was a good man, well respected in our town and established as a business man. His family had been close to ours for years. And although I didn't know him well (he was 14 years older than me!), I trusted my father's good judgment.

Our wedding was beautiful. I'll never forget our first night alone in the bedchamber. I trembled as Eliud wrapped me in his warm embrace and whispered, "Samantha, ours will be a home overflowing with laughter! We'll have a dozen sons and daughters bouncing off of one another. We will be rich with love and good times!"

I nestled into his arms and once again dreamed of babies; lots and lots of babies.

A year later, Eliud brought me fresh flowers. He placed them in the vase on our table, drew me to himself and with a twinkle in his eye, he asked, "Sam, do you know how many flowers are in that bouquet?"

"Hmm..." I looked at the beautiful flowers and started to count.

"No, that's cheating!" Eliud laughed.

With his strong arms he lifted me off the floor and swung me in the air. "Sam! There's a full dozen plus one! And that's how many children we will have soon."

I wanted to laugh with him; Eliud was always optimistic and his faith was strong. But, already my body hadn't conceived even though we'd been married for a year. I wondered if something were wrong. Still, many couples waited two, even three, years before their first child was born. It was way too early to worry yet. So, I giggled softly with my good husband and smiled at his confidence.

Just a few months later I knew we were pregnant. We were expecting the first of our dozen plus one children! Jehovah God had heard our prayers and was smiling on us.

I wanted to surprise Eliud with the news, although a small part of me enjoyed having this secret all to myself. I prepared his favorite meal and gathered my own bouquet of 13 flowers and set them in the center of the table. As I heard Eliud's steps on the path to our door, I took one last look at the special dinner I'd prepared. Then I quickly ran to the bouquet, took out a single flower and placed it on Eliud's plate.

Eliud embraced me like he always did right as he walked in the door.

"I have some news for you," I whispered as I kissed his ear.

"Hmmm. Good news I hope!" Eliud winked at me.

"Very good news. But let's eat first!" I replied.

I could hardly contain myself as I led him to the table.

Eliud caught his breath, "Somebody's been busy! What's this? Sam..."

His eyes grew large, and he looked at me with so much hope I knew all my hard work was paying off. Eliud slowly counted the flowers in the vase, then picked up the single bloom I'd placed on his plate.

"Are you...are we...?" He couldn't get the words out.

"Mmm, hmm. I am, we are!" I laughed at his speechless stupor!

What a celebration we had that night.

My baby was growing in me. I felt him move and kick. I spent more time stitching baby clothes and less time cleaning. I was careful to eat just right and get plenty of rest. All was going so well. My world couldn't have been better.

But then, my baby stopped moving. The first day I wondered if I were simply being too anxious. I tried to reassure myself. "Really, Sam, don't be a worry wart!" I'd say. Then after the second day came and went without any movement, I told Eliud.

Always the encouraging man, Eliud assured me this had to be normal but he'd call the physician just in case. The physician came. He poked, prodded, listened to my belly, then he quietly folded his bag and sadly told Eliud and me that this baby had died.

"No!" I cried. Eliud shook his head sadly and squeezed my hand. Then, he walked the physician out of the house. They whispered as they went.

"No, no, no!" I cried. I held my belly and tried to will this baby back to life.

Eliud returned, sat by my bed and in a low hoarse voice he said, "Sam, I have to tell you something."

A tear ran down his cheek. I don't think I'd ever seen Eliud cry.

I searched his face for any hope...any at all. Eliud always chose to see the bright side of every situation!

"The physician said you are in grave danger. The baby in you could kill you. You have to drink this. It will make you sick. The sickness will make the baby come. When you deliver the baby, you will begin to get well. You will get well."

Eliud's strength and confidence seeped into his broken heart. He looked me in the eyes and said again. "Sam, you *will* get well."

I drank the bitter tea. Almost immediately I became terribly sick. I tossed in my bed. When the contractions came, they were severe. The labor lasted two days. The midwives bathed my forehead with cloths, and they quietly rubbed my hands as they silently waited the birth of my dead son. He was born in the middle of the night. There was no celebration. Only silence. They quietly wrapped him in old rags and took him away. They didn't even let me see his face. I cried. Oh, how I grieved. My arms longed to hold life, while my body shuddered from the death it bore. Eliud was not allowed to see me that night; my life was still in danger, and only the midwives came near. They told me I was in and out of consciousness for a week. When I awoke, I was so weak I stayed in bed for a month. Gradually my strength returned. The physician checked on me and told me that the bleeding should stop within the next few weeks. He said that when that happened I was free to gradually resume my chores.

Eliud was quiet. We both were trying desperately to deal with our shared loss. But when the bleeding continued another month, I begged Eliud to find another physician. Surely there was something that could be done! I wanted life to return to normal so we could start working on those babies. I'd known women who'd survived similar losses and gone on to have large families.

Eliud reluctantly found another doctor. This one came from a nearby village. He was young and confident. He examined me and prescribed another herbal tea. I shuddered to think of drinking another unknown herb. But he assured me this tea would make me well. So, for another long month I sipped his herbs. But still my bleeding continued.

Eliud asked my sister to come live with us. Sarah was a great help to us. She cooked Eliud's meals and kept his house. Sometimes I heard them laughing as they were sharing their meals together, and I wondered if he'd be happier with her. Please don't get me wrong. Eliud never once gave me reason to be jealous. He was faithful to me. He still sat by my bed and read Scripture to me in the evening. But I worried that I was no good for him.

After six months I cried uncontrollably. Sarah begged Eliud to find another doctor. She told him that I was not eating and couldn't even talk. My head throbbed, and my stomach ached from so many tears. I couldn't stop crying! I stopped drinking the tea. It didn't help, and I wondered if it somehow triggered the tears.

Another doctor came to our house. He assured my husband that he knew of a new treatment, but that it was very expensive. Eliud told him that money was not an issue. He was willing to spend whatever it took to stop my bleeding. The doctor promised us that his new treatment would work. I'm not exactly sure what the doctor did; he made me smell something strong and I went to sleep. I only knew that when I awoke the terrible cramps were worse than ever and my bleeding continued strong.

After a few days of heavy bleeding, it began to subside. I told Sarah to help me up. Together we wrapped me so that I could move around even as I continued to bleed. I felt so dirty and so alone. But I refused to stay in that bed. Though my bleeding never stopped completely, the treatment lessened it for exactly three months; then the old pattern re-emerged: cramping, clotting, flowing, continual pain, continual discomfort, no relief, and total weakness. Even getting dressed took several hours, as I had to pause to rest—or fall back in bed for fear of fainting. Every day my head ached. I had to make myself eat. I was always short of breath. Eliud spent more time at work and less time with us. I missed the good times we used to have. This pattern of life continued for years.

I watched sadly as all my friends gave birth to several children. I heard cheerful shouts, laughter and even tears of children who lived nearby. No one knew what to say to me, so they simply avoided me all together. Except for Eliud and Sarah, I had no friends at all. Even my other sisters and brothers were busy with their families, and they felt awkward around us because our home was terribly void of the fullness of life. I was daily accompanied by my salty tears and the constant flood of life flowing out of me. I longed for life to grow in me, but instead it seeped out ever so slowly, day by day. This continued for years.

At first I fussed and fumed. I shook my young fist at the sky and demanded that Jehovah give me an explanation for my affliction. But with His great silent response, I gradually stopped shaking my angry fist. I started talking to Him like I'd never talked to Him before. I told Him how deep I felt the loss of my son. Then I told Him how grateful I was for Eliud's unshakable love for me. Of course there were no other flower bouquets, and neither of us ever mentioned the single bloom I'd laid on his dinner plate.

Eliud never teased me anymore, and he never mentioned children around me. He respectfully gave up our marriage bed and made himself a pallet on the roof. I missed his body next to mine, but with my infirmity, that was not even thinkable.

I asked God to heal my body. I asked Him every day. He didn't so much as offer a rumble in the distance to acknowledge that He'd heard my cry.

One night Eliud paraded through the doorway and across the room; he came straight to me and planted a kiss on my forehead. "Sam, I've met a man who can make you well." He spoke with the old confidence and even with a hint of the old joy we used to share.

"Oh, Eliud, so many men have tried. What makes this man different?" I tried not to sound too negative, but really, what else could men do?

"This is not an ordinary man, Sam. His name is Jesus, and He's traveled all around healing the lame, giving sight to the blind. I heard He even brought the son of a widow back to life!" Eliud exclaimed.

In my mind I thought, "I wish He'd been here when my son was dead."

But to encourage Eliud, I asked, "Have you spoken with this man, Jesus?"

"No, but I heard He's on His way here. Let's go, Sam. Let's go see Him!" Eliud was so full of enthusiasm that I almost forgot God doesn't care! What harm could it do? Maybe if we just got close enough to see Him heal others, I might conjure up some hidden hope. "OK, I'm game, Eliud. For you, I'll go see this man called Jesus."

We found Him near the synagogue. I hadn't been to church in years. I was ceremonially unclean, and if the Pharisees knew I was in their midst in my condition, they would reprimand me severely. I shuddered to think of the possibility. I huddled close to Eliud and clung to his arm for support. Jesus was telling stories, interesting stories. The people were quiet, captivated by His words. We hid in the back of the crowd. Many people knew of my infirmity, and they would scatter if they thought they might come in contact with me.

I watched as He held children in His lap. He tenderly caressed them and said, "unless you become like this little child, you will not enter the kingdom of heaven!" Then He talked about a mustard seed. I'd seen the mustard plant. It is huge! The correlation Jesus was making was the vast difference between a tiny mustard seed and the crop it produces. I listened closely. He encouraged everyone to have faith—to believe in God. He spoke as if He were God. I couldn't help but wonder. Jesus was not like any other man I'd ever seen. Eliud nudged me, "Sam, let's go up there."

"No, I can't do that! These people, they'll be horrified if they find out I've been in their midst! Please Eliud, now is not the time!" I begged him to leave me be. Reluctantly Eliud stayed with me, and Jesus gave the children back to their parents. He walked right past us, within arm's distance away. I could hear Him talking quietly with His disciples, and could practically feel the warmth of His body as He passed. A crazy thought crossed my mind; it was almost like a voice in my head: "Touch Him, just reach out and touch Him."

I shook my head and ignored the voice. I didn't know all of who Jesus was or why He was able to perform such miracles, but I did know He was a holy man. And I couldn't dare touch such a man with my unclean hands.

Eliud and I walked back home without saying a word. We were both thinking about our encounter with Jesus. He was remarkable, that was for sure. I hoped to see Him again, and anxiously waited for Eliud to come home and tell me we were going back. But the next day Eliud told me Jesus had sailed away on the lake. There was such a storm that night that I couldn't help but whisper a prayer for His safety. He was gone for months.

The story about the mustard seed continued to play itself over and over in my head. I felt like a little tiny seed of hope had been planted in my heart. I found myself looking for Jesus every day. Somehow I began to believe that if I could just see Him again, my prayers of the past 12 years would be answered. I even plotted how I might convince Eliud to somehow make contact with His disciples and beg them to come to our house. I'd daydream about it—Jesus walking through the doorway, coming right up to my bedside, placing his hand on my forehead and speaking softly, "Arise, my love."

Then I would give up on that possibility when I considered what a holy man He was. How could I ask such a man into my unclean home?

I forced myself out of bed and talked Sarah into taking walks with me. In order to stay away from the crowds, we walked by the shore. I pretended to be drinking in the fresh air, but actually I was searching the horizon for Jesus and His disciples. Since this was the way He left, I hoped it would be the way He would return. It was on one of these walks that we headed toward the shore and my heart skipped a beat. A large crowd was gathering; could it mean that Jesus had returned?

Yes! Jesus and His disciples were in the middle of the mayhem. All that happened next is still a blur. Without thinking, I pressed into the crowd, until I was right up close to Jesus. He was talking to a Pharisee. Jairus' daughter was obviously ill. The proud Pharisee didn't seem so proud right now. He knelt at Jesus' feet and pleaded with Him to come to his house. Jesus lifted him up, looked him in the eyes and assured him He would come right away.

My heart froze. Jairus was living my dream! Jesus would go to his house and heal his daughter! It's not that I didn't want that to happen; it's just that suddenly I felt an urgency in my spirit. If I didn't somehow make contact with Jesus at this moment, I would never know His healing power. So, I pressed even closer. I nudged my way through the crowd—I had only one thought in my mind, "If I just touch His clothes I will be healed." He wouldn't have to come to my home. He wouldn't even have to stop on His all-important mission of healing Jairus' daughter. If I could just get my hands on the hem of His robe, my bleeding would stop!

And there I was. He was right in front of me. I smelled His salty hair. I heard Him giving instructions that only a few of the disciples were to enter Jairus' home with Him. And, then someone bumped me from behind. I knew it was now or never so I reached out as I started to fall and I barely caught a tiny bit of His robe with the tip of my fingers. Just before I hit the ground I knew I was well. The cramping that had been so familiar immediately stopped; the bleeding ceased. My head cleared, my strength was restored, and the pain and weakness disappeared in the moment. I knew at once that not only was I completely well, I was clean too! I felt cleaner than I'd ever been! I couldn't move. I was frozen in place, time stood still. People pressed all around me; soon they were between Him and me. I wanted to shout, I wanted to dance, and I wanted to sing! I wanted to bow at His feet and say, "Thank You, Lord!"

Suddenly the crowd stopped moving, silence filled the air. Jesus spoke in an authoritative voice, "Who touched my clothes?"

He looked around, searching the crowd. His disciples responded, "Can't you see all these people crowding in around you? So many have touched you, how can you ask 'who touched me?'"

But Jesus peered into the crowd. He searched each face.

I shrunk back. Unexpectedly my joy turned to fear. Apparently Jesus felt something when I touched His robe. I didn't know He *felt* my need. How could He *feel* me touch Him? I only barely caught the hem of His garment! What would make Him identify with me to such a degree? Was I in trouble? Did I hurt Him? Did I steal His power without asking? Oh my, I didn't mean to do that; it's just that I knew He could...He would heal me if I could simply touch His robe! I didn't want to make a scene. What would all these people think?

Jesus refused to move. My heart grew to the size of a cantaloupe and leaped to my throat where it beat like a drum. I stumbled forward and fell at His feet. I buried my face in the dirt. There I confessed, "It was me, Lord. I knew You would make me well." I tasted my tears mingled with dust as they fell on His feet.

Jesus placed His gentle hand on my head. He lifted my face to look Him in His eyes. The crowd remained strangely quiet, as I looked into the face of a man who knew me already. It was as if we'd talked to one another for years. Immediately I realized I was in the presence of God. He was answering my years of prayer. He didn't send a rumble in the distance; He sent His precious Son who healed my disease.

"Daughter, your faith has made you well," He said.

Somehow I knew He'd heard me all those years I'd prayed. Somehow I knew He'd been listening all along. Now I'd already figured that Jesus and God were closely linked. But when I saw the familiarity in His eyes, I decided they were one and the same. While these thoughts filled my freshly cleared mind, He added, "Go in peace and be freed from your suffering."

I wanted to thank Him with words, and as they were taking shape in my mouth, some men came from Jairus' house and interrupted our sacred moment. Immediately Jesus' attention returned to the desperate man. I knelt there speechless as they hurried on. In hopes of getting another chance to express my gratitude, I followed them.

We arrived at Jairus' home where the mourners were already assembled. They cried loudly as was proper for a Pharisee like Jairus. His little girl was dead. I hurt for Jairus. I wondered if my reluctance to step forward quickly when Jesus stopped His urgent mission to meet my need cost the little girl her life. I felt a twinge of guilt rise in me. But Jesus rebuked the mourners. He said, "The child isn't dead. She is only sleeping!"

My apprehension was immediately replaced with anticipation of what

Jesus would do next! Being paid mourners, they scoffed and laughed at Him. I shook my head in unbelief. Why couldn't they believe Him? This was God Almighty telling them the truth!

We waited while Jesus, a few of His disciples and Jairus went into the girl's room. In no time at all, the little girl came skipping out the door hand in hand with her mother. I laughed and cried all at the same time. She was 12 years old. Exactly the same age my little boy would have been had he been born so long ago. She represented all the years stolen from me by the issue of blood that racked my body. I allowed her laughter to fill my heart, and I felt 12 years of joy restored. I knew God was with me all those years; He sustained me, and now He'd healed me. I completely forgot about thanking Jesus face to face. I suddenly remembered Eliud and his faithful love. I had to go find him and share my joy—our joy!

We lived a happy life. Our house was filled with children and is now full of grandchildren. I thanked God again and again for healing my body. I knew I could talk to Him; I'd already been talking to Him before I ever met His Son face to face. God blessed me with twins, and I was pregnant with their little sister when we heard they'd crucified my Lord. I wondered at the madness of that but later discovered it was all a part of His plan. Now we tell our grandchildren about our heavenly Father, and they watch Grandpa Eliud's eyes sparkle as He tells them of how Grandma came face to face with Jesus when He walked the earth. I tell them how I felt when He tenderly called me "Daughter." We tell them they can be His sons and daughters too if they'll just have faith like a mustard seed.

Questions for Reflection

1. How did Jairus' faith compare to the woman who was healed by touching Jesus' robe?

2. How does pride impact our ability to believe God?

3. What is faith?

4. Do you have a faith challenge? How can you demonstrate faith in this situation?

5. Did Jesus come to remove suffering on the earth?

6. What is our job when people around us suffer?

7. How does knowing *God does the work of God* impact the way you view and participate in ministry?

8. Has God ever allowed an interruption in your life for His glory?

Ask God To

- Remind you of your comforting ministry when loved ones suffer.
- Be glorified in your life as you choose to trust Him with your greatest burden.
- Do His work in and through you this week.

MY PRAYER FOR THIS WEEK

A VERSE TO MEMORIZE

If we confess our sins, He is faithful and just
and will forgive us our sins,
and purify us from all unrighteousness.

—

I John 1:8

CHAPTER 5

Caught!

WOMAN TOUCHED BY JESUS
The Woman Caught in Adultery
John 8:1-12

INTRODUCTION
"I Am Responsible for Me"

I remember the first time I was caught speeding. I was leaving the seminary campus, hustling to the bank so I'd be back in time for my afternoon class. I suppose the culprit was the afternoon class. I never liked afternoon classes because my body has always rebelled against doing anything mental after noon! I can rise early, greet the sunrise, have my quiet time, exercise, take a shower, feed my family, answer email, write thank you notes and catch up on my phone calls all before noon. But after noon, if I sit still, my eyelids grow heavy, my brain waves calmly drift into gentle ripples, and if I'm sitting, I'm soon catching a few moments of much needed "shut eye." If I'm up and moving, I'm ok. The sleep only makes its sneak attack when I'm sitting down. So, the way I see it, I wouldn't have been hurrying to the bank if I hadn't had the afternoon class. However, I got caught because I was going 50 mph in a 35 mph zone. It didn't matter that everyone else always went 50 mph there too. What mattered was that I was breaking the speed limit (by 15 mph) when the policeman happened to be patrolling.

What a terrible place to get caught! The officer pulled me over to the side of the road on the main thoroughfare for seminarians as they travelled to work, lunch or Braum's ice cream parlor. (And all seminarians went to Braum's!) I wanted to cry, in fact I did, but my tears meant nothing to him. Nor did he care that I'd never had a speeding ticket before. He didn't bat an eye when I promised I'd never go that fast again. He wasn't even impressed when I assured him I was a good Christian girl who had committed her entire life to God's kingdom work and happened to be poor because I'd chosen to attend seminary rather than work full-time when I graduated from college. He simply wrote me a ticket, wished me a fine day and left me in my puddle of humiliation.

In this chapter you will visit with the woman caught in adultery and consider the impact sin has on your life. It is my prayer that you will learn to embrace conviction and chastisement from the Holy Spirit. I pray also that you will learn how to deal with the guilt that sometimes lingers long past God's forgiveness.

DAY 1
I AM RESPONSIBLE FOR ME

Read John 8:1-4

Caught in the Very Act

The Bible tells us that the woman caught in adultery was caught in the *very act*. Now, just imagine that for one minute. She wasn't caught because she talked to the wife of a Pharisee and reluctantly admitted her illicit affair with a man who wasn't her husband. She wasn't discovered because a snoopy religious leader somehow confiscated her diary. This woman was caught in the *very act* of adultery. There is ultimate humiliation in being caught in the midst of your sin. Can you remember being caught in sin? Where were you? What sin were you caught in?

> *If we confess our sins,*
> *He is faithful and just*
> *and will forgive us*
> *our sins, and purify us*
> *from all unrighteousness.*
> I John 1:8

What did it feel like to be caught? How did you respond to being caught?

Meet God in His Word

Read Genesis 3. This chapter tells the story of sin's entrance into our world. What did Eve do when she was caught in sin?

How did Adam respond to God's question about his sin?

Often our natural response to being caught in sin is to pass the blame. Even in my introduction to this chapter, I blamed my afternoon seminary class for my speeding ticket! It is human nature to pass the buck, to cast blame on someone or something else. If we can't blame anyone, we'll start justifying our actions. How often do you lose your temper and justify it by saying, "If she hadn't talked back to me, I wouldn't have yelled." Or, "If he'd realized what a difficult day I'd had, he would have been more sensitive and I wouldn't have been grumpy."

The decision to sin begins and ends with you. Who was punished for Adam and Eve's sin?

Although God cursed the serpent, He didn't allow Satan to take all the blame for sin. God carefully, meticulously, lovingly shaped Adam and Eve to be His companions. When He created us in His image, He placed in us the freedom of choice. With freedom comes responsibility. God held Adam and Eve responsible for their own free will. They could not expect the serpent to take all the blame for their sin because they chose, of their own free will, to listen to his lies and give into his temptation. Bottom line is that you have to take responsibility for you. You cannot blame anyone else for the sin you choose to get yourself tangled in. No one else is responsible for getting you out of your mess. You are responsible for you.

A serious problem in our society today is the lack of personal responsibility. Parents expect childcare providers to take full responsibility for their child's health and well-being. Patients expect their doctors to take full responsibility for their health or the lack thereof. And the cost of malpractice insurance skyrockets because doctors expect their insurance companies to take responsibility for their mistakes. The list could go on and on...parents expect educators to not only teach academics but morals and character development as well. We look to the courts to determine right and wrong, we look to teachers to wipe out illiteracy, and we expect welfare to wipe out poverty. Our prisons are full of men and women who blame other people for their crimes. Our homes are full of estranged families who blame one another for their miserable relationships.

Please don't get me wrong. I know there are terrible, unspeakable things that happen to innocent people. If we live long enough, all of us will experience injustice. But even people who've been wounded by others must take personal responsibility in order to be released from the anger, fear, resentment and harm done to them by others. When will we accept the fact that we are each responsible for ourselves?

I am responsible for me, and you are responsible for you.

Face to Face with Jesus

Write that fact in the space provided. Print: I am responsible for me.

Now, what does that mean? Have you cast blame on someone or something else? If so, who? What did they "make" you do?

How can you accept full responsibility for your sin? What changes do you want to make as you begin to apply the truth that "I am responsible for me"?

Ask God to show you how you can take full responsibility for you. Ask Him to reveal any blame you've cast on others. Ask Him to show you any way you've tried to justify your sin. Allow God to cleanse your heart as you humbly ask for His forgiveness. Don't miss the fact that when we confess our sins, God not only forgives us, but He also purifies us from the power of that sin. Thank God for giving you the power to conquer sin in your life. At the end of your prayer time, read aloud I John 1:8.

"If we confess our sins, He is faithful and just to forgive us of our sins and purify us from all unrighteousness."

MY PRAYER FOR TODAY

DAY 2
THE MINISTRY OF THE HOLY SPIRIT

Read John 8:1-8

God Is Love

Yesterday was a difficult lesson. I hope the experience triggered the Holy Spirit's work in your heart. Anytime you deal with sin and guilt, you must base all your understanding of God on the cross.

"For God so loved the world that He gave His one and only Son, that whoever believes in Him shall not perish, but have eternal life. For God did not send His Son into the world to condemn the world, but to save the world through Him." (John 3:16-17)

I John 4:16 says "God is love."

The nature of God is love. Sin separates you from the perfect love of God. Jesus bridged the gap created by sin by paying sin's penalty—a cruel, sacrificial death on the cross. The perfect Lamb of God took away the sins of the world. Sin no longer separates you from God. Exercising your free will to choose or reject Jesus' gift of salvation is now the only thing that separates you from the love of God.

> *If we confess our sins, He is faithful and just and will forgive us our sins, and purify us from all unrighteousness.*
> I John 1:8

Meet God in His Word

Let's pause right now for just a moment. If you do not know peace with God, if you do not know for certain that you will go to heaven when you die, you can know right now. Carefully read the following verses and answer the questions:

Romans 3:23—Who has sinned? What did that sin cause between you and God?

131

Romans 6:23—What is the cost of sin? What free gift does God offer?

Romans 10:13—What is required in order to be saved?

Romans 10:9-10—What two parts of your body must you use in order to be saved?

Did you say that you must confess with your MOUTH and believe in your HEART? If so, you are absolutely right. God loves you with perfect love. God is also dead set against the sin that separates you from Him. He will not allow His holiness to be compromised by your sin. Therefore His perfect love provided the perfect price for your sin. Jesus died on the cross to pay the penalty for your sin. Then He rose from the grave demonstrating God's victory over death and reassuring us that He can and will make good on His promise of eternal life. Do you believe this is true? If so, pray this simple prayer:

Dear God, I know that I am a sinner. I take responsibility for me. I've done wrong things. I believe Jesus died for my sins. I also believe He rose again and lives today. Please forgive me for my sins, come into my heart and take me to heaven when I die. Be the Lord of my life. In Jesus' name I pray. Amen.

If you prayed that prayer just now, call a friend and tell her. Because you have confessed with your mouth that Jesus is Lord and believed in your heart that He rose from the dead, you are saved. The angels in heaven are rejoicing right now over your salvation. You are eternally saved to live in peace with God forever.

For many of you who are reading these words, you've already prayed that prayer. Do you remember that day? Write down your memories of the time when you asked Jesus into your heart and life:

Revelation 3:20 says, "Here I am! I stand at the door and knock. If anyone hears my voice and opens the door, I will come in and eat with him, and he with me."

Your salvation is the greatest miracle of all. When Jesus supernaturally comes into your life, He becomes part of your every day. He plants His Holy Spirit in your heart; and when you choose to obey Him, talk to Him, walk with Him, read His Word and live according to it, His influence in your life expands. But, you still have to make the choice daily. God gave you free will. He will never overstep His boundaries established by your freedom. Jesus always stands at the door and knocks. He waits for you to open your life to Him. He never pushes His way in.

This presence of God *in* us is called the Holy Spirit. Read John 16:5-15. Jesus gives the Holy Spirit a descriptive name in verse 7. What is it?

Jesus told His disciples that when the Holy Spirit comes He will do one main thing. What is it?

He will _____ the world of guilt in regard to sin, righteousness and judgment.

What other descriptive name did Jesus use for the Holy Spirit? (v. 13)

What does the Holy Spirit do for us today? (v. 15)

...the Spirit will take from what is mine and make it _____ to you.

Face to Face with Jesus

When you allow the Holy Spirit to convict you of guilt, you are entering into a holy place. Without conviction there can be no salvation. Without conviction there can be no release. Without conviction there can be no peace.

Thank God for convicting you of sin when you first asked Him to forgive you of your sins, come into your life and take you to heaven when you die. Thank Him for the joy that replaced your guilt.

When you allow the Holy Spirit to speak God's truth to your heart, you are experiencing the power of God working in you. This is not a one-time experience. The Holy Spirit reveals truth to you and convicts you of sin on an on-going basis. Allow God to convict you of sin even today. Ask Him to forgive you, then thank Him again for forgiving your sins, ruling in your life and taking you to heaven when you die.

Let the joy of the Lord be your strength today as you celebrate the fact of I John 1:8.

MY PRAYER FOR TODAY

DAY 3
THE OLD THINGS HAVE PASSED AWAY!

Read John 8:9-11

Unwritten Rules of Conduct

For the first seven years of being a pastor's wife, I chose to embrace these three unwritten rules of conduct.

- Rule #1: Don't be too friendly with your parishioners. (They may stab you in the back.)
- Rule #2: Don't ever talk about your husband as if he were a mere man. (They need to believe he's bigger than that.)
- Rule #3: If you mess up and break rules 1 or 2, paint your house and list it for sale. (It's time for a new field of service.)

Tom grew up in a parsonage and, therefore, understood the wisdom behind this code of conduct. He didn't have a problem with my strict adherence to my three rules! However, during the years I lived by them I missed the privilege and abundance of sharing God's authentic love with the people in my faith family. Through a series of painful experiences God taught me to toss "the rules."

First there was infertility. My mother lives four and a half hours away; and as I privately suffered through endless tests, procedures and basal body temperature charts, I grew lonely. I needed encouragement. I needed a few friends—girls I could confide in, laugh with and cry with. One day as I was writing in my prayer journal, I actually thought I heard God tell me to testify to His goodness toward me even in the midst of my pain. So, the next Sunday morning I told our entire congregation about our three-year ordeal with aggressive infertility treatment. There wasn't a soul in the congregation

> *If we confess our sins, He is faithful and just and will forgive us our sins, and purify us from all unrighteousness.*
> I John 1:8

who knew I'd had surgery some months before. But when I obeyed God and allowed myself to be honest and vulnerable, women who could identify with me wrapped me in their arms. Others who could not identify with me seized the opportunity to love on us. The prayers for our children multiplied after that Sunday morning.

I swallowed my pride and let them in. This was not easy to do, but over time I grew to trust them. When God blessed us with our daughter Mikel, the entire church family rejoiced over her birth. Tom and I enjoyed the spotlight when our little congregation threw us the ultimate baby shower. God's abundant blessing continued to flow (three babies in three years). And out of desperation I let the women come closer—even into my home. One friend took it upon herself to teach me how to be a stay-at-home mom. We laughed and cried together while she walked miles up and down my hallway, consoling my colicky little Kaleigh. When my schedule grew hectic, she even cleaned my bathrooms!

This was huge for me. Self-sufficient, independent Leighann let women come through her strong defensive wall, and it was OK! In fact, I enjoyed breaking my rules. I broke every one! I didn't worry about pretending to be perfect. I didn't worry about putting up a shield; I started enjoying the company of women in the church. We went on retreats; we went to the beach. We took "ladies nights out." I grew to love these women.

Remember rule #1? Don't get too friendly with your parishioners; they may stab you in the back. It's true; they did. By the time Kaleigh was potty trained, the same friend who'd held her and scrubbed my toilet, told me she and several others thought Tom was a liar. It was a sunny Sunday afternoon, and we were standing in the hall of the church next to the small foyer table (the one that held fresh veggies in the summer free to anyone who would take them). She spit her words into the air, and my delicate crystal ornament created from years of dreaming what it might be like to fulfill the role of pastor's wife came crashing to the floor. That ornament shattered into a million pieces and was beyond repair.

I was hurt, but that was only the beginning. Over the next year accusations continued to fly. It seemed to me that every woman I'd befriended now stood as my accuser. They and their husbands hosted secret meetings. Our church was torn by gossip and backbiting. It all ended with the exit of 60 + people. All my close girlfriends were gone. I was beyond hurt; I was devastated. Little voices crept into my head: "See there, you should've stuck to those rules!" I even painted our house (rule #3) over the weekend Tom visited with the staff and pastor search committee of another church.

But God didn't call us away from our church. Tom bounced back with great resilience. God was doing something new, and Tom *knew* it. In the months following, our church exploded with growth. The Holy Spirit mended our corporate wound and pressed us forward. New people stepped up to positions of leadership left vacant by those who'd chosen to leave. And ever so slowly I tried to glue my crystal ball back together. I couldn't do it. Everyone around me was happy and all was going well, but still I hurt. How could I ever again open myself up to the women of the church?

Bitterness and resentment filled my heart; and I was afraid that if I let them go, the void created would leave me vulnerable and defenseless. It was through the ministry of two prayer partners that God taught me to love and trust again. He gradually replaced my hurt with peace. I digested the truth that God is love, and if I wanted to love God, I had to love people too. I realized that love hurts, but love keeps loving. The Holy Spirit kindly confronted me with the things I'd done wrong during those years, and I had to ask God to forgive me for those things. Then I had to let God remove the guilt those regrets left behind.

After some time I chose to love again. I chose to be real again. I chose to leave the masks behind and allow God to be my strong defense. God blessed me as I chose these changes. Several women came and asked for my forgiveness. Ever so humbly I allowed God's forgiveness to flow through me. I was the one who was humbled by their willingness to ask! The friend who held my Kaleigh never returned. We've seen each other since and have been cordial and friendly. And I can honestly confess that God restored my love for each one of those who hurt me back then. But He taught me more than that. God allowed me to understand the He is the one who loves perfectly. And as I allow myself to be a vessel of His love, I am not crippled by the hurt that may come my way.

Since that time so many church members have come and gone and come again that I can't keep up with it. I don't carry a crystal ball anymore. My image of being a pastor's wife is now more like those super bouncy balls my children get when they turn in their tokens at the pizza/party/pandemonium place they used to beg to go. My bouncy ball won't break, and when it falls (as inevitably it will), it has one incredible bounce on the way back up! I have a more realistic view of what it means to be a pastor's wife. I choose to be real. I don't expect everyone to treat me like a queen. I choose to be reminded that I and my husband are merely dust. I'll be the first to warn others not to think of us otherwise. And, I don't paint my house. We've been here nearly 20 years. If and when God gets ready to move us, He can sell this house "as is."

I told that story to remind you that you can't allow your present to be clouded by your past. God allows all sorts of difficult situations. Some of them are none of your doing; some of them are your own fault! Either way God intends to work good in us through all these things!

"And we know that in all things God works for the good of those who love him, who have been called according to his purpose." (Romans 8:28)

Meet God in His Word
One of the first verses I memorized after I invited Jesus into my life was 2 Corinthians 5:17. Turn there in your Bible and underline this verse:

"Therefore, if anyone is in Christ, he is a new creation; the old has gone, the new has come!"

According to this verse, what happened to the old?

Why then do so many of us continue to let our today be affected by yesterday?

Face to Face with Jesus
God has method to His management in our lives. While Romans 8:28 assures us of God's ability to work good in all things, verse 29 tells us that God's intent is to conform us into the likeness of His Son. He often uses difficult situations, persecution by others, any number of hurtful—seemingly harmful—circumstances to press us into the image of Christ. So, would you allow God to show you how He aims to redeem your past and turn it into good as He molds you into a reflection of His Son?

Ask God to show you which "old things" you choose to carry around with you. Agree with Him that those things create a heavy load. Let Him lift that load from you. Offer yourself as clay to the potter. Let Him use the things you've just given Him to mold you into the image of Christ.

MY PRAYER FOR TODAY

DAY 4
"I AM A PERSON OF WORTH..."

Read Ephesians 5:1-21

Who I Am...in Christ

My parents gave me a loving Christian home. They taught me to dream big dreams. When I was in the eighth grade, I ambitioned to be the first female president of the United States! But somewhere in my childhood, I embraced a bold faced lie, and even today I have to kill it daily. That lie said, "You are of no value, Leighann. You are ugly; your best effort is not good enough; you will amount to nothing." Every once in a while this lie was validated by someone's cruel teasing or by my own failure. When I was in the tenth grade, I started my political career. I ran for sophomore class secretary. I misspelled secretary on all my campaign signs and didn't even notice my mistake until our English teacher made an example of it in front of the class! "Your best effort is not good enough, and you will amount to nothing!" I heard the whisper in my ear.

> *If we confess our sins, He is faithful and just and will forgive us our sins, and purify us from all unrighteousness.*
> I John 1:8

Needless to say, my brief political career ended in an embarrassing defeat. I don't know why I've struggled with this lie, but I do know that buying into it cost me dearly; and as I grew up, it unfortunately became a driving force toward looking to others to receive endorsement of my self-worth.

I asked Jesus into my heart when I was 11, and He immediately went to work to eliminate this toxic way of thinking. My first year at youth camp the summer after seventh grade we studied a book titled, *Self, You Bug Me!* written by Grady Nutt. The week was built around one sentence from that book. Ever since that week of camp, I've used the same sentence to kill the lie that haunts my toxic thinking patterns. Here it is:

I am a person of worth created in the image of God to relate and to live.

You are God's idea.

As I continued to navigate through the white waters of adolescence, I came to grips with God's opinion of me. The night I asked Jesus into my heart, the deciding factor was the value God placed on my soul. He spoke in His powerful voice to my heart and allowed me to understand that if I had been the only one in the entire world who chose to sin He would have still sent His Son to die for me. That meant I was valuable to Him.

I grew in my relationship with God and realized that I was created in His image. Image is an interesting phenomenon in our culture. Magazines show us pictures of people who spend their entire lives preparing their bodies to be photographed, and their images are still enhanced by computers! We purchase these magazines, then we try desperately to choke down the cabbage soup diet on page 132, only to be sorely disappointed when our thighs failed to get thin in thirty days!

That is the image of beauty. But then there is also the image of success. Success is making lots of money and proving to men that we can do what they can do—only we can do it better! Or maybe success is sacrificing all that money can buy, dedicating yourself to your home, grinding your own wheat into bread and home schooling your quiver full of children!

God is not looking for beauty or success. He's looking for mirrors. We were created in His image. When God looks at us, He wants to see Himself in our eyes. What does that mean? How can we reflect the image of Christ?

Meet God in His Word

In Ephesians 5 Paul writes that we ought to be imitators of God as dearly loved children. He then goes on to remind us that God is love, and, therefore, we should live lives of love. Just in case you're wondering what kind of love God requires of us, Paul reminds us that God is looking for us to live lives of *sacrificial* love. When we sacrifice out of our love for God, we become a fragrant aroma to His heavenly senses. (By the way, the Old Testament teaches that when we whine, we are a stench.)

Think about that for a moment. We have the ability to impact heaven with a fragrant offering much like the woman who anointed Jesus filled the room with her fragrant perfume. When we love one another, we become a fragrant aroma to God. We bathe Him with glory.

But let's get back to the part where Paul tells us we ought to be imitators of God. One of the joys of parenthood is watching your children grow. Several times Tom and I have commented about how amazing it is to see both of us reflected in our children. Mikel, Kaleigh and TJ all three have characteristics that reflect mine and Tom's image in their lives.

Maybe our three children are like us because they're made of our DNA. Maybe they are like us because they spend so much time with us. Maybe they are like us because they admire us and want to be like us! Maybe!! I don't know exactly how Mikel, Kaleigh and TJ are getting to be such a mixture of Tom and me, but I do know they give us a great illustration of Paul's instructions in Ephesians 5:1. In the same way Mikel, Kaleigh and TJ reflect characteristics unique to me, and unique to Tom, so God wants us, His dearly beloved children, to reflect His characteristics in our lives.

God's already done the miraculous work of making us His sons and daughters. When we asked Jesus into our hearts, God placed the Holy Spirit there. Paul tells us in another letter to the Corinthians that God gave us His Spirit as a deposit, a guarantee of our eternal life to come. We were "born again." God allowed us to be born of the Spirit; He placed His spiritual DNA in our hearts.

Now we must do our part. As we spend time with Him by studying His Word and praying, we'll become more like Him. As we choose to admire Him and allow His characteristics to intentionally be put into practice in our lives, we will become more like Him.

Face to Face with Jesus
Do you buy into lies that attack the image you embrace for yourself? There's no room for poor self-esteem in God's kingdom work. If we're esteeming ourselves, we're looking in the wrong mirrors! Our attention is on the wrong "god." God longs for us to take our eyes off the world...off ourselves...and off other people. He's urging us to turn them on Jesus. If you know this song, sing it:

Turn your eyes upon Jesus, look full in His wonderful face
And the things of earth will grow strangely dim in the light of His glory and grace.

Tell God that you will embrace Grady Nutt's sentence and that you will take initiative to be like Him today: *I am a person of worth created in the image of God to relate and to live.*

MY PRAYER FOR TODAY

DAY 5
"THOSE WHOM I LOVE I REBUKE"

Read John 8:1-11

Discipline

Discipline. I don't like it. When I first wrote this, I was sitting in my office located in the detached garage apart from the house. It was early in the morning, and I was "hiding" from my family. Here's what I wrote:

I know I should go back over there and prepare breakfast for the children, but there will be weeping and wailing in the McCoy home this morning. Dad's been preaching a revival out of town this week and drives back home late at night. When he keeps these hours, he warns Mikel, Kaleigh and TJ to behave while he's gone. Most of the time they behave well. But this week they haven't. What started Monday as just little spats and a few episodes of talking back escalated on Tuesday to major temper tantrums and sassy tongues. Amidst tears and negotiations, I stood firm and assured them that this time I would indeed report their behavior to their father. I added that he would most likely punish them first thing in the morning. (Not a very nice way to say, "good night," but I have to draw the line somewhere!) Even as I write, I know they are curled in their beds dreading the wrath of their father they know is inevitable.

> *If we confess our sins, He is faithful and just and will forgive us our sins, and purify us from all unrighteousness.*
> I John 1:8

I just don't like it. I'd rather greet them this morning with pancakes and strawberry milk and say, "Let's just forget the whole thing. You be good today!" And in my imaginary world they will smile at me, hug one another and heartily agree that this is a new day and they can be different. Only, that will never work. The pain inflicted with discipline is the only way their actions will change. I've tried all of my mothering years to allow grace to supercede judgment, but they often take full advantage of my grace and continue pressing the limits until discipline is administered. Somehow the pain speaks truth they can't hear any other way, and they are miraculously transformed back into the precious children I know and love.

God understands this dynamic. He made us and, therefore, knows how best to rear us. Jesus introduced us to the concept of God as our loving Father. Jesus paid the penalty of our sin and ushered us into the family of God. In Galatians 3 and 4, Paul reminded us that we are now sons and daughters of God. With that privilege comes responsibility. When we become God's sons and daughters, He takes His role as Father seriously in our lives.

In Ephesians 2:10 Paul tells us we are God's workmanship. In other words we are His projects. He examines His progress daily in our lives. And He meticulously shaves away what does not belong, all the while shaping what is developing well. God uses discipline to do this.

As parents we do the same thing. We examine our children's progress daily. Tom and I have goals for our children. We intend for our three to be productive, content, God-fearing, Jesus-trusting disciples of Christ committed to lives of service and devotion. Discipline is probably the most important part of that process.

I was an art minor in college. In art appreciation, I decided that my favorite artist was Michelangelo. And one of my favorites of his works was his portrayal of David carved out of stone. Michelangelo's David looked just like I'd always envisioned David to look. I've heard it said that someone asked Michelangelo how he took a piece of stone and created something so marvelous. He told them it was easy really; he merely chipped and chiseled away everything that didn't look like David.

That is what God's discipline does. Discipline chips and chisels away everything in us that doesn't look like Jesus. Remember, God's goal for us is that we would be reflections of His Son.

Meet God in His Word

Read Revelation 3:19 and fill in the blanks:

Those whom I _____ I rebuke and _____.

If you've ever felt the wrath of God in your life, you can be assured of His fierce love and devotion toward you. God disciplines those He loves.

Look back at that verse again. How are we to respond to the discipline of God?

So be _____ and _____!

Now read Revelation 3:20-22.

God is our loving Father. I think He cries when we cry. I think He cries even when He disciplines us. God does feel like our parents told us they felt, "Please know, this hurts me more than it hurts you!" (I never actually believed them, still don't.) But God loves us deeply. He grieves over our sin; He weeps over our despair. Even when He disciplines us, He stands at the door of our hearts, He knocks and He longs to come in. He promises great reward on the other side of discipline if we would just repent—lay down our pride and our stubborn rebellion.

Face to Face with Jesus

I'm learning so much about the love of God by being a parent. Christmas is just around the corner. We celebrate the holidays with gifts and surprises. I enjoy being Santa as a mother even more than I enjoyed receiving from Santa as a child. Even now I'm plotting my strategy for ways to fill the holidays with fun and excitement for my children. I look for just the right toys. I have to wait until Thanksgiving at least for my children to begin mentioning what their hearts are set on getting. Just like many of you I search for the bargains, and I get up at 5:00 AM to take advantage of the early bird specials. If it were left up to me, I'd give my children every single silly plastic pleasure their little hearts are yearning to receive. But, I have a goal in mind for my three. I intend for my children to be productive, content, God-fearing, Jesus-trusting disciples of Christ committed to lives of service and devotion.

So, I shop in moderation. I think of their lack of gratitude and their attitude of "I deserve this!" I wish they would be naturally grateful. I wish they'd wake up on Christmas morning and say, "Oh Mama, let's rejoice in Jesus' birth before we unwrap our gifts! Let's read Luke 2 and sing a few carols!" I wish they weren't so me-centered and were more God-centered. And then I think of my heavenly Father and I wonder if He has to shop in moderation for me as well.

God has abundant riches just waiting to pour out on you and me. He longs to give good gifts to us. But, because He has a goal in mind for us—He intends for us to be reflections of His Son—He waits...He watches...He examines our hearts for signs of gratitude, and He gives to us according to the measure we are capable of receiving. Sometimes His lack of giving is His way of disciplining. Always what God chooses to give or withhold...what He chooses to permit or to take away...is used to mold us, make us...to chip and chisel away anything that does not look like Jesus in us.

Thank God for loving you enough to discipline you. Ask Him to have His way in your heart as you yield it to Him.

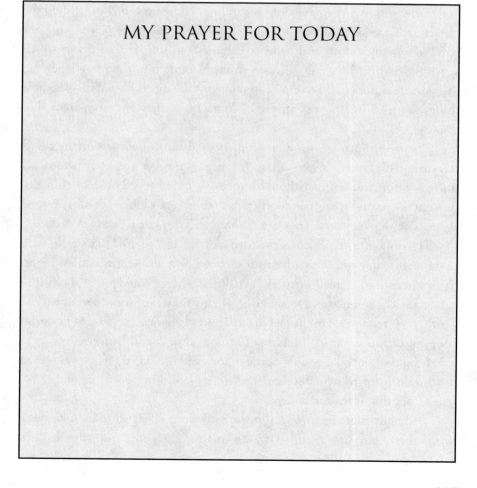

MY PRAYER FOR TODAY

From the Heart of the Woman Caught in Adultery (A story based on John 8:1-12)

I knew it was almost dawn. The birds were just beginning to sing outside my window. Oh, to have a song in my heart and to sing boldly without a care in the world. I longed for such freedom. But from the time I was young, I knew only shame and remorse. A long time ago, I'd known joy and true happiness. Like any other little girl, I gathered wildflowers and dreamt of my future husband, a happy family and children. I gently rocked my baby brother and snuggled close to his peachy soft head. I smelt his baby sweetness and wondered if I'd have a baby boy or a baby girl first.

But then my uncle came to visit. He was so fun; the twinkle in his eye and the attention he gave me drew me to him. How was I to know he had the capacity for such evil? When he came to me in the night, he placed his giant hand across my mouth and whispered harshly in my ear that if I so much as whimpered he'd have me thrown from the cliffs into the place where all the garbage smoldered. I dare not so much as breathe as he did unspeakable things to me. When he was finished, I knew I was dirty...so dirty—stained to the core.

The next morning was a blur. All I could remember was my mother's scream and my father's anger. Oh, such anger as I'd never witnessed before. My uncle ran from our house without his robe. My father yelled obscene things as he went. But worse than that, mother and father never looked at me the same again. They looked away. They were ashamed. They knew I was stained.

The sun began to peak over the corner of the night. I used to love this time of day, a new day with new adventures. Now I only wished for endless night, night where nothing really mattered. Darkness where I could put my body into mechanical obedience and steal perhaps a tiny morsel of some sort of wicked worth. I was reconciled to the fact that delivering physical pleasure to powerful people was the only thing I had to offer. It paid well, and I survived.

I could still smell the foul odor of onions and fish. He'd obviously enjoyed his dinner prior to his after-dinner exercise. I couldn't even remember his name...not that it mattered anyway.

Suddenly there were voices outside my door. They sounded like men, lots of them. He cursed, pulled the covers from the pallet and stumbled out the back. I sat up stunned as the men burst through the door and pressed in toward me. They stood staring at me while I groped for anything to cover myself. Any one of them might have sought my services in the dark of the night. But here in full daylight they huffed, and scoffed, in disgust, as they stared at my nakedness. I was so ashamed.

With a pompous shout the leader of the men said, "Woman, you will come with us! God will deal with your sin today!"

Trembling I surveyed the room. There was no escape. The men were at both doors, and they were not about to budge. I winced as two of them stepped forward and grabbed my arms in a grip that made my heart give up any hope of mercy. As the two jerked me from the pallet, yet another shoved my robe to my chest nearly knocking me off my feet. I don't remember putting it on. They drug me from the house, and I scraped my shins when I tripped over the door frame. Bruises were forming on my arms, where their fingers dug into my flesh, and I looked at the ground.

I wonder what stoning feels like. I wonder if they'll knock me out first with a large rock to the head and mercifully let me lay unconscious before I die. Or will they pelt me with little rocks, bruise every inch of my body and make sport of me? I wonder if dying hurts as bad as living this shell of a life I've lived. All these thoughts rushed through my mind.

Eyes...I couldn't get the eyes out of my head. Men never looked at me with warmth. Their eyes always communicated one of two things: savage hunger or arrogant disgust. Last night and so many nights before, their eyes filled with savage hunger. Today and so many days before, it was arrogant disgust. Suddenly I was shoved to the ground. I dare not look up, but as I studied the dirt, I felt the eyes of many looking down at me.

"Teacher, this woman was caught in the act of adultery. The law of Moses commanded us to stone such women. Now what do you say?"

Teacher, did they say "teacher"? I'd heard of this teacher. My cousin Rachel told me all about Him.

"You need to come meet this man they call Jesus!" she said.

"Oh, come on. He can't be so different than all the other men!" I'd answered back.

"No, Becca, (Rachel was the only person in the world who still called me by my childhood nickname, short for Rebecca), this man is different! Just wait until you see his eyes."

"I've seen men's eyes. They hold hunger that is easily satisfied with flesh, or they hold disgust that is only satisfied with shame. I've no need for the eyes of men." I responded.

"Becca, all I know is that this man is different. His eyes are full of compassion, and I've only seen Him heal with His hands. Please come with me to where He's teaching today." Rachel pleaded.

"Not today." With that the conversation ended.

But here so close to what I thought would be the end of my life, I couldn't resist the urge to peek at this man. Timidly I lifted my eyes and glanced over to the one they called, "Teacher." He wasn't so big, and His clothes were not fancy—unlike the men who'd paraded into my house this morning. He was surrounded by common people; men, women and even children were sitting right up close to Him. He sat with dignity and seemed to be in the middle of deep discussion when He was interrupted by their presentation.

I couldn't see His face, only His body as He bent down and started drawing in the sand. What was He doing?

"What do you say? The very act! We caught her in the very act! She was still in her sin-filled bed when we found her!" My accusers went on and on.

But He continued to draw in the sand. Was He ignoring them? What was He doing? I admired the way He refused to be upset by their interruption. Finally, He stopped. He straightened up and said to them, "If any one of you is without sin, let him be the first to throw a stone at her." Then he stooped down again and continued writing in the sand.

I wondered at His answer and almost chuckled to myself at His calm response to what was obviously a trick question. Now I knew why these arrogant religious hypocrites hated Him so. I sensed the power of His authority that would not be coerced into playing their religious games. Knowing their arrogance, I still fully expected the stoning to begin any second...so I merely smiled at His clever answer and braced myself for the first rock.

After a few seconds of silence, I noticed the oldest man sigh deeply and shuffle off away from the others. This started a quiet exit one by one of all my accusers. I watched in amazement as they walked away in silence. Before long I was the only one still standing. I'd had my head down in shame the entire time, wishing for something in which to hide my face. Unfortunately, in their haste, the religious leaders had only grabbed my robe to cover my nakedness and hadn't even thought to provide a covering for my hair. Suddenly I felt very much alone. I lifted my head expecting Him to look at me with eyes filled with righteous indignation and judgment.

But as I lifted my face, I heard Him say, "Woman, where are they? Has no one condemned you?"

With the first glimpse into the perfect love of Jesus, my cousin's description came flooding back to me. Rachel wasn't kidding! I had never seen such compassion and total acceptance as those eyes held. All my sin, all my shame—my past hurts, my wrong choices, my guilt—all of it was there, standing before this purely holy righteous man. And although I knew my sin was plastered all over me, somehow His eyes reflected only complete, unreserved total acceptance and love.

I answered, "No one, sir."

I couldn't take my eyes from His. Before words ever formed in His mouth, I knew whatever He said, He meant. And as I marveled in His glory, I heard Him say, "Then neither do I condemn you. Go now and sin no more."

More precious words had never been spoken.

Questions for Reflection

1. What does it feel like to be caught in the very act of sin?

2. Why do we play the blame game?

3. What must we do in order to be freed from the vicious cycle of destruction in our lives?

4. How can you take full responsibility for your sin?

5. Share how you felt the day you confessed your sin to God, invited Jesus into your life and believed Him for salvation.

6. Why is conviction a good thing?

7. What does God want to do with our past?

8. How much value does God place on your soul?

9. When God disciplines us, He has a picture of what He wants us to be? What does that picture look like?

Ask God To

- Bring conviction for the sin He sees in your heart.
- Give you courage to take responsibility for you.
- Open your heart and mind wide to understand the depth of His love for you.
- Teach you to embrace His discipline, recognize it and yield to it.

MY PRAYER FOR THIS WEEK

A VERSE TO MEMORIZE

He who did not spare his own Son,
but gave him up for us all—how will he not also,
along with him, graciously give us all things?
—

Romans 8:32

CHAPTER 6

Begging and Receiving

WOMEN TOUCHED BY JESUS
**A Woman Who Begged and
A Woman Who Didn't Even Ask
Matthew 15:21-28 and Luke 7:11-17**

INTRODUCTION
"Begging and Never Asking"

When I first read about these two women I wondered, why did one mother have to beg Jesus to heal her daughter while another simply watched Him resurrect her son from the dead without even asking Him to do so? I still wonder.

There have been times in my life when I felt like the woman who had to beg Jesus for even the "crumbs that fall from the master's table." I have other powerful answers to prayers I never even knew to pray. I dare say you most likely have prayers in both these categories as well. By visiting with these two women, we will consider how we ought to respond to both situations. We will establish one basic premise:

God is good, all the time.

We will determine the truth of this statement in God's Word and in our own lives. Then we will learn how to build our entire faith journey on that firm foundation. We will be challenged to pursue Jesus like the woman who begged for crumbs, and we'll learn to rejoice like the woman who received a miracle she didn't even think to pray for.

Our memory verse will remind us that God is always for us because God is good, all the time!

DAY 1
"AH HA MOMENTS" AND "POP QUIZZES"

Read Matthew 15:21-28

Ah Ha Moments and Pop Quizzes

When you participate in a study like this, God graciously gives you "ah ha moments," then He follows those with "pop quizzes." At the exact time I was writing these lessons, I was faced with a pop quiz. I was spending hours at the computer urging us to focus on the deeply personal relationship God longs to share with us. I even wrote a day's lesson on how Jesus never experienced interruptions in His schedule. And then life happened. Mikel (my then 6th grade daughter) had gotten behind on her schoolwork. Since we were home schooling (the first semester of her 6th grade year), I took full responsibility for her education. All of her academic assignments were on computer software. On Wednesday night, I took her computer to church to use for Power Point in the prayer study I was teaching, and although I brought the computer back home, I failed to include the power pack and electric cord. Her laptop would only run for two hours on battery. So, late Thursday morning on my way to a lunch appointment, I had to go out of my way and swing by the church to fetch the computer accessories.

> *He who did not spare his own Son, but gave him up for us all—how will he not also, along with him, graciously give us all things?*
> Romans 8:32

When I arrived at church I saw a woman who had been crying. She was talking with our education pastor. He introduced us and said, "This is a divine appointment!" To which I smiled on the outside, but inside I was screaming, "No it isn't! I don't have time for divine appointments!" I was not thinking of the woman healed from her 12-year issue of blood (and how her encounter with Jesus only seemed like an interruption in His schedule). I just wanted to gather my things and be on my way. However, I urged my "divine appointment" to come with me to the choir room and told her we could talk and pray as we walked. I did take time to sit down and pray with her, and was graciously empowered by God to minister to her. Before we said "amen" I was overwhelmingly convicted that ministry has to be people focused! How dare

I ever get so busy that I plow over hurting people in my path. Hurting people are my ministry! They are your ministry too.

I don't know if I passed or failed my test. Maybe I earned a "C." You can decide. Perhaps Jesus was giving His disciples a "pop quiz" when He ignored the cries of the Canaanite woman. Unfortunately, His disciples acted without compassion, and that is not at all what Jesus wants us to do.

Meet God in His Word

What happened when the Canaanite woman first came to Jesus? Why do you think Jesus ignored the woman?

What was the disciples' response to the woman?

We know that Jesus was not prejudiced. We established that fact when we saw Him interact with the Samaritan woman at the well. Jesus not only offered her living water, but He also stayed in her town for a few extra days to share His message of eternal life with other Samaritans who lived nearby. So, why didn't Jesus respond to the Syro-Phonecian woman? Maybe He was watching to see how His disciples would react to her.

I can't help but wonder how the disciples could be so "dull." (Jesus used this descriptive word in verse 16 when He explained a parable regarding cleanliness and tradition.) When Jesus seemed to ignore the Canaanite woman, He might have been giving the disciples an opportunity to apply what He'd just taught. In Matthew 14:1-20 Jesus offended the Pharisees because His disciples were caught eating without washing their hands. Jesus told the Pharisees that they too broke God's command by adding to the commandment to "Honor your father and mother" a clause for their own personal advantage. He went on to call them hypocrites. Then, Jesus made a public spectacle out of the Pharisees by using this situation to teach the crowd that what comes out of a man is what makes him unclean—not what goes in.

This could have been an "ah ha" moment for Jesus' followers. If their hearts were receptive, the Word of God could have broken the chains of tradition. Second Timothy 3:15-16 says the Word of God is living and active. I hope that you have many "ah ha" moments as you participate in this study.

I've discovered that sometimes just after these "ah ha" moments happen in my quiet time, my newfound understanding is put to the test. Perhaps Jesus was setting His disciples up for a pop quiz by ignoring the Canaanite woman's cry for help.

The Canaanite woman (like the Samaritan woman) would have been considered "unclean" to devout Jewish men. She would be considered a Gentile and, therefore, unworthy to receive anything from God (according to Jewish tradition). Would Jesus' disciples encourage Him to show compassion toward her (regardless of her ethnic background), or would they turn her away (because of their deep rooted tradition)? Read verse 23. What did the disciples do?

Face to Face with Jesus

Jesus' disciples failed the quiz. Apparently they never considered how desperate this mother was. Obviously they didn't envision the suffering of her daughters' demon possession. Instead they complained that she was bothering them! How aggravating is that?

"Lord, this woman keeps on following us, crying and hollering...Jesus, please send her away!"

Thank God for giving you pop quizzes to follow your "ah ha" moments. Ask God to open your spiritual eyes so you will see hurting people today and be ready to greet them with compassion.

MY PRAYER FOR TODAY

DAY 2
WHAT TO DO WHEN GOD DOESN'T SEEM TO BE LISTENING

Read Matthew 15:21-28

Infertile Prayers

When I was struggling with infertility, I prayed. I prayed every day that God would give us a baby. I begged. I pleaded. I even wrote little notes to God that looked like this: "Dear Lord. I love You and believe You can make me pregnant this month. Will You please give Tom and me a baby? Circle one: Yes No."

No kidding! I really wrote that in my prayer journal. A few weeks later I circled "no." For three long years God seemed to be ignoring me. I wondered if He cared. The months marched on, and He seemed not to mind that I was desperate and longing. But when He seemed silent, I continued to go to Him. I stayed in His Word, and I clung to His promises.

> He who did not spare his own Son, but gave him up for us all—how will he not also, along with him, graciously give us all things?
> Romans 8:32

Before God ever answered my prayer for a baby, He let me in on what He was doing during the time I thought He was ignoring me! In actuality, He had His undivided attention on me! God was stretching me and growing me. He was teaching me things about Himself and revealing to me things about myself I would have learned no other way. God was tenderly molding, shaping and making me into the person He wanted me to be.

God allowed me, just like the Canaanite woman, to demonstrate my faith. Here I am today 16 years removed from my infertile experience, and God is still using that story to speak His truth to others. Here we are 2,000 years removed from the Canaanite woman's encounter with Jesus, and God is still using her experience to speak His truth to us. God is good all the time!

Meet God in His Word

Did Jesus send the woman away like His disciples asked Him to?

No! Instead, Jesus engaged her in conversation. "I was sent only to the lost sheep of Israel." This was an interesting thing for Jesus to say. What do you think He meant?

How did the woman respond to Jesus' statement?

She now had His undivided attention, and she was not about to lose it! I wonder how long she followed them crying and begging. She had to have followed Jesus for some time; otherwise the disciples would not have complained about her. But once Jesus addressed her, she demonstrated incredible humility, perseverance and faith by kneeling at His feet and saying a simple thing, "Lord, help me!"

Think about that prayer. "Lord, help me!"

Have you ever felt like praying such a prayer? Have you been so desperate for God to work powerfully in your life or in the life of someone you love that you simply cried out, "Lord, help me!?" When? How did God respond to your prayer?

Read verse 26. How did Jesus respond to the woman's prayer? Fill in the Blanks:

It is not right to take the _____ bread and toss it to their _____.

Who was Jesus referring to when He made reference to the children? Who was Jesus referring to when He made reference to the dogs?

The "children" referred to the children of Israel. The "children" were the descendents of the promise, the chosen ones—those whom God loved and longed to have relationship with. They were the Jews—those whom God disciplined, those whom He rebuked and those whom He'd promised a Messiah. Until Jesus taught otherwise (and until Peter and Paul realized God's love included Gentiles too), God was seen as the God of Israel.

The "dogs" referred to everyone else. Anyone who was not a Jew was a Gentile. Most of us would fall in the "dogs" category. The Canaanite woman knew exactly whom Jesus was referring to when He mentioned the dogs. Read her reply in verse 27. What do dogs do? What was this woman willing to do?

Perhaps this is why Jesus called the Canaanite woman's faith "great." She was willing to be satisfied with Jesus' leftover "crumbs" of compassion and miraculous power. For she knew in her heart that even His leftover "crumbs" would be enough to satisfy her deep longing—to fulfill her desperate need.

Face to Face with Jesus

What about you? Do you approach Jesus with this kind of faith? If He seems not to listen, would you be willing to keep crying out until anyone close to Him might be tempted to say, "Send her away, she won't be quiet!" If He challenges your right to petition Him, what will you say? Do you understand that even the crumbs from the Master's table are enough to answer your heart cry?

Thank God that we are not considered dogs to Him. Thank Him that we are His precious children. Thank God for the truth He's given us about this unique relationship we share in Romans 8:32.

MY PRAYER FOR TODAY

DAY 3
GOD IS GOOD

Read Matthew 15:21-28

God's Goodness Revealed to Moses

As God was forming the nation of Israel, He revealed Himself to them. Moses had a unique relationship with God. He was God's chosen leader of the Israelites—the one who took them out of Egypt and toward the promised land. Moses spoke to God "face to face as a man would his friend" (Exodus 33:11). God and Moses had many conversations as God led the people through the desert and used those years to shape them into a nation that would declare His glory to the world.

More than once God grieved over the lack of faith demonstrated by the Israelites' disobedience. After the golden calf incident, God told Moses He wouldn't go with them to the promised land, but instead He'd send an angel. This upset Moses. He interceded on behalf of the people and prayed, "Lord, if Your Presence does not go with us, do not send us up from here. For only Your Presence makes us different from other people in this world." God relented and agreed to go with Moses and the people all the way to the promised land. Moses felt such a great love for God at that moment that he asked God, "Show me Your glory." Moses already had a unique relationship with God, but even as intimate as they were, Moses yearned for more. He wanted to see all of God. He wanted to understand God and His ways. Moses wanted to experience all of God's glory.

> He who did not spare his own Son, but gave him up for us all—how will he not also, along with him, graciously give us all things?
>
> Romans 8:32

God agreed to allow Moses to glimpse His goodness. But He warned Moses that no man could see His face and live. So God pointed out a place in a rock where Moses would be safe and agreed to allow His glory to pass by the rock. God assured Moses that He would cover Moses' face with His own hand until it was safe to look.

You can read this story for yourself in Exodus 33.

In the next chapter God did what He said He would do. After Moses chiseled two more stone tablets from rock and left for Mount Sinai early in the morning, God came down in a cloud and stood in front of Moses. Then God proclaimed His name.

Meet God in His Word

Turn to Exodus 34: 6-7 and read how God described Himself to Moses. List all the characteristics God used to describe His glory:

Did you find seven? Compassionate, gracious, slow to anger, abounding in love, abounding in faithfulness, maintaining love to thousands, forgiving wickedness, rebellion and sin. When God talks about Himself, this is who He says He is. This is the self-portrait God gave to Moses to share with His people.

> God is compassionate.
> God is gracious—slow to anger and abounding in love and faithfulness.
> God maintains love to thousands.
> God forgives wickedness, rebellion and sin.

> God is good.

Many times God's people chose to ignore His goodness. Because they chose to forget who He is, their interpretation of His activity in their lives grew distorted. Their lack of faith in the goodness of God blinded them to His love for them. Their lack of faith hindered God's activity in their impossible situations. The Old Testament is full of situations where doubt gave way to despair. However, the Old Testament is also filled with situations where faith gave birth to prosperity and victory!

Face to Face with Jesus

If you don't start from the foundation of the goodness of God, difficult times will come and you will be tossed by waves of doubt. Basic to your faith is receiving the truth that God loves you with perfect love. You must evaluate all God's activity in your life against the backdrop of His perfect love.

Go to Matthew 15:21 one more time. What does the Canaanite woman call Jesus? Which characteristic of God does she appeal to? (Fill in the Blanks.)

_____, Son of David, have _____ on me!

God's mercy is never-ending. His goodness compels Him to want only what is best for you. What about you? Are you tempted to believe God doesn't care? Do you listen to voices of doubt? There is one verse in the Bible that wipes away any ounce of doubt regarding God's love toward you. That verse is Romans 5:8. Print it in the space provided:

Thank God for His description of Himself. Tell Him you believe He is compassionate, gracious, slow to anger and abounding in love and faithfulness. Tell Him you know He maintains love to thousands and forgives wickedness, rebellion and sin. Thank God for demonstrating His own love toward you. Be like the Canaanite woman, appeal to Him because He is your Lord and base your appeal on His mercy.

MY PRAYER FOR TODAY

DAY 4
"DON'T CRY"

Read Luke 7:11-17

Don't Cry

Today and tomorrow we're going to take a look at another woman who received Jesus' miraculous touch. This woman didn't even ask for Jesus' help; she merely wept in her own distress. Without a son, this widow had no hope. She would not have anything like the life she might have known when her husband and son were living. Widows were at the mercy of others. They were as helpless and hopeless as orphans. What did Jesus say when He saw this woman?

"Don't cry."

When do we say those words? Do we say them when we know something the person crying does not know? Do we sometimes say them when we know we can do something to make that person feel better? Perhaps we also say those words when we know their pain will eventually get better as they grow to see the bigger picture!

> *He who did not spare his own Son, but gave him up for us all—how will he not also, along with him, graciously give us all things?*
> Romans 8:32

Today is November 3, 2003. It is a red-letter day on our calendar because Kaleigh (my 10-year-old daughter) got to change her earrings today. She's been looking forward to this day for six weeks. Ever since Kaleigh was six, she wanted to pierce her ears. I intended to make her wait until her 12th birthday—but then gave in to her pleading and decided 10 would be a good birthday to celebrate with pierced ears. We went to the mall on her exact birth date, September 22. She was so excited. For the past six weeks we've cleaned her ears with antiseptic. Kaleigh got accustomed to sleeping with her earrings in her ears. Then all last week she counted the days until Monday, November 3. First thing this morning Kaleigh took out her original earrings. Then she lost the back to a new pair of earrings. Amidst her tears I said, "Don't cry!" I explained to her that any back would fit her new earrings and surely we could take care of that.

No sooner had I taken care of her first tears than another fresh round of tears greeted me. This time Kaleigh had accidentally dropped her pearl earring down the bathroom sink. Again I urged her, "Don't cry!" But this time I was not sure if we could retrieve her earring. I assured Kaleigh her father could help us, and sure enough Tom took the sink apart and presented Kaleigh with her tiny pearl earring (a birthday gift from her "Mammer"). While Tom was being the plumber, I went to Kaleigh's room and helped her find the back to the earring that she had dropped earlier. All was well! Kaleigh successfully changed her earrings!

Twice I said to Kaleigh, "Don't cry!" The first time I knew something she didn't know. I knew you could wear any back with any earring! The second time I told Kaleigh "Don't cry" I hoped Daddy would recover the earring from the drain. That time I encouraged Kaleigh to hold off on her crying to give him a chance to see if he could.

Jesus told the woman, "Don't cry." He said this to comfort her. He said this to encourage her. Jesus told her to stop crying because He knew something she didn't know.

Meet God in His Word

Read verse 14. What did Jesus do as soon as He told the woman to stop crying?

Face to Face with Jesus

Do you ever feel like your situation is so desperate that all you can do is cry? If you do, crawl into your heavenly Father's lap and listen for Him to say, "Don't cry." Then watch what He'll do next. Thank God for caring for you. Read Psalm 56:8. The NASB says it this way,

"Thou hast taken account of my wanderings; put my tears in Thy bottle; Are they not in Thy book?"

God collects your tears! Not one of them escapes His notice. Thank Him for loving you so, and ask Him to wipe them away...every one. Don't forget, God knows many things you don't know, and He can fix your hurts.

MY PRAYER FOR TODAY

DAY 5
JESUS CARES

Read Matthew 15:21-28 and Luke 7:11-17

Glorious Answers to Desperate Pleading

I called my infertility specialist on day 38 of my cycle. We faithfully tracked my basal body temperature on charts during those years. Usually my temperature took a dip a day before menstruation would begin. That was always my warning that we'd failed once again to get pregnant. This particular month I was mostly positive we weren't pregnant. I'd gone to Ridgecrest, North Carolina, to participate in conferences the week I ovulated. Tom stayed home. When I returned home I scheduled an endometrial biopsy because the doctor wanted to perform it during a time when we felt confident we were not pregnant. The biopsy itself was invasive and could upset the environment for a developing baby. During an endometrial biopsy the doctor could even inadvertently scrape the baby from the uterine lining. We were confident that our fertile days came and went without being together, so I thought it was the perfect time to get this test behind us.

> *He who did not spare his own Son, but gave him up for us all—how will he not also, along with him, graciously give us all things?*
> Romans 8:32

I was eager to receive the results of the biopsy, and the doctor could not interpret them until my menstruation began. We were all waiting for that to happen. For the past three years my cycle began between days 30-34. So, on day 38 when my temperature remained high and my cycle had not yet begun, I called the office. Sharon, (my nurse) recommended that I come in for a pregnancy test.

I'll never forget the conversation, "Sharon, my temperature is still high and I haven't started. I'm pretty eager to know something about that biopsy. Is there anything we can do?"

Sharon replied, "Leighann (long pause), I think you should come in for a pregnancy test."

"A what?" my heart started beating fast. "Why should I do that?"

"Well, that is what we've been trying to do all this time, isn't it?" Sharon responded.

"Yes, I know, but do you really think we could be pregnant?" I was afraid to even hope!

"Yes, I think you could." Sharon seemed almost as excited as I was.

I drove to the office during my lunch break. I prayed all the way. "Dear Lord, You know how we've talked about this so many times. I'm not sure I am ready to handle the disappointment of a negative test today. Please prepare me for whatever is next in this journey. You know I love You, and I am committed to Your best for our life. Please, please let me be pregnant and give us a baby. Please!"

All the way there I was like this Canaanite woman. I had God's undivided attention, and I just wanted to whisper, "Lord, help me!"

The office was closed for lunch, but they knew I was coming; and Sharon greeted me from the break room where she, another nurse and the receptionist were eating their sandwiches. She gave me the little cup to collect my urine and sent me to the bathroom. I passed my cup through the window in the bathroom and prayed as I got ready to meet her for the results.

"Lord, this has been quite a journey. Please...is this it?"

I walked to the door of the break room, and Sharon greeted me with the plastic test, "Leighann, you're pregnant!!"

Everyone in the break room shouted. We hugged one another and laughed and cried. I made Sharon explain to me how she could be so sure. She gave me that precious little test and showed me the definite blue dot on the side where such a dot indicated the positive presence of the pregnancy hormone. I was speechless. I'd come to this place every month sometimes more than once for the past three and a half years. Our goal was always to get me pregnant, but that goal had become so unattainable that I'm not sure I ever really thought I would experience that moment. I bumbled through some silly questions like, "What do I do now?" (to which Sharon answered by giving me the name and phone number of a good obstetrician), thanked them all and walked back to my car.

As I drove down the ramp to the interstate, I talked to God again, "Thank You...oh thank You! How could I ever be so blest to experience Your enormous power directed toward me. Thank You! Oh, God..." And then I lifted my heart in sheer praise that words could not even contain. God...had been silent for so long...then He heard my voice, He heard my cry for mercy!

My friend, God hears you, too. He chooses some times to linger when

He answers your heart cries. But don't ever allow the lingering time to cause you to forget...Jesus cares!

God is good, all the time.

Meet God in His Word

Briefly review these two stories. Do you feel like the Canaanite woman? Is there a prayer you've been praying that seems to be ignored? Are you searching for God's response to your desperate cry? If so, underline the following promises in your Bible.

Jeremiah 31:25	Let God satisfy you right now.
Psalm 145:8-9	Thank God for His graciousness and mercy.
Psalm 147:3	Allow God to heal your wounds right now.

Claim these verses as you lay your cause before Him once again. Ask God to replace your longing with confidence in His perfect love.

Face to Face with Jesus

If you do not have a desperate cry today, think of a time when you experienced God's answer to a prayer. Take a minute to reflect on how His love and power amazed you at that time. Write a prayer of thanksgiving to God.

How many times has God reached down from heaven and given to you before you ever even thought to ask? Can you list some of the many ways God's chosen to bless you?

Did your list include your health, your home, your financial resources, your ability to work, your spouse, and your children? Did you include the air you breathe and the bed you sleep in? God is always providing for us. Often He gives us more than we even know to ask for, simply because He loves us.

Tom and I now have three beautiful, healthy children. Mikel, Kaleigh and TJ are normal kids who are growing daily. So many days I take their health and maturity completely for granted while God continues to pour His blessing all over their lives.

Tom and I have served God through the ministry at Thompson Station Church ever since January 1989. Through the years, God has blessed our church beyond what words can describe. Not a week goes by that we don't receive an email from one who has experienced the power of God active in their life. Not only that, but where Thompson Station was once a tiny rural community, it is now one of the fastest growing areas in Tennessee. Only God could put us smack dab in the middle of such an exciting mission field. We didn't even know to ask Him to do this! When we approached seminary graduation, we just wanted to be where we could fulfill our call. This too I take for granted all too often yet God keeps on expanding our territory, and increasing our joy.

The list could go on and on. The many blessings of God that I never think to ask for. There are times when He provides me a Psalm that says, "I know where you are and exactly what you're thinking." Sometimes He sends me a song in a worship service or a note of encouragement. They never stop coming my way, little reminders that He is on the throne, anticipating my need and putting the universe in motion to provide more than I could ever ask or imagine.

God does that for you too.

Thank God that He is good all the time. Thank Him for the promise of His word in Romans 8:32.

MY PRAYER FOR TODAY

From the Hearts of the Woman Who Begged and the Woman Who Didn't Even Ask
(A story based on Matthew 15:21-28 and Luke 7:11-17)

The Woman Who Begged

How was I to know they had come here to rest? Not that it would have mattered to me anyway. I didn't want to nag. I certainly didn't intend to be a bother; it was just that...oh, let me start at the very beginning.

When Natalie was only three she started acting strange. I'd find her staring into thin air. I'd try to distract her, but her brown eyes were far, far away. Some days she'd act like a normal little girl, chattering and laughing...but then other days she would be tormented by some unseen evil force. She'd awake in the middle of the night screaming. I'd go into her room and she'd be drenched in sweat, her clothes stripped into shreds. She'd hurl things at me as she uttered obscenities she had no way of knowing. I was frightened and didn't know what to do. I'd try to reassure her with soothing words, but as she grew older she was too strong for me to restrain. We had to use ropes and tie her to her bed. Oh how I'd weep over my little girl so lost and confused. There was nothing else we could do. If we didn't tie her down she'd hurt herself or someone else! I'd stand outside the door and wait for the torment to stop.

When the spirit left her, the room grew quiet. I'd slowly crack the door open and peak inside. She'd look at me from the prison we'd locked her in and with fear-filled, confused eyes she seemed to say, "Mama, why are you doing this to me?"

Natalie was 10 when I heard He was coming into our region. He never came here. Most of the time He ministered near the Lake of Galilee. But word of His miraculous power had spread. We heard of how He healed the deaf man and straightened the woman's back. We heard all about the woman who was released from seven demons! Each time I heard someone give an account of what they'd seen Him do, I just knew He had the power to help my daughter. I was working on a plan to take Natalie to Him. I didn't know how I'd manage it, since my husband was dead and my other relatives and friends were unwilling to risk untying her ropes. I have to admit that I was even scared of her when the demon manifested itself. I wept, I prayed, and I grieved over my inability to bring relief to my suffering little girl. I wondered what I'd done wrong for God to punish me so.

But then I heard He was on His way here. Someone had seen Him traveling with His disciples. I didn't even think to consider that this was not a mission trip for Him. Not that I thought it was...all I knew was that Natalie needed Jesus and I had to do what I could to get His attention. So, I sat by the roadside and waited. I saw Him while He was still a long way off. He was traveling with several men and even a few women. I heard them laughing as they walked. There were about 15 or 20 of them in all. Although I'm normally a quiet reserved woman, I was pressed into action by the echo of Natalie's screams I could still hear in my head. As soon as I knew they could see me, I stood in the middle of the road, waved my arms wildly and yelled, "Lord, Son of David, have mercy on me! My daughter is suffering terribly from demon possession."

From everything I'd ever heard, all you had to do was tell Him your problem and He was more than willing to take care of it. I'd heard how He stopped on many occasions and took time to heal diseases, forgive sins and cast out demons. He'd done this in places other than Galilee. I knew if He'd done it for the man in the Gerasenes, surely He'd do it for my little girl. My heart beat strong in my chest, and my voice never wavered. I was about to receive my miracle!

But as they approached me, He didn't say a word! He didn't even look my way. I thought perhaps He was so deep in conversation that He hadn't noticed me, so I yelled louder, this time adding a little jump to my arm waving.

Some of His disciples glanced my way. One looked me in the eye, then he turned to look at Jesus. Because Jesus never slowed His step, nor did He nod in my direction, this disciple merely shrugged his shoulders and walked on more quickly. I continued to yell. I walked up close to another of them, pulled on his sleeve—and pleaded. He paused, wrinkled his brow, then muttered something I couldn't understand and jerked away. I wondered at how this magnificent man could be surrounded by such "Jewish" people! The Jews always looked down on the rest of us. They somehow considered themselves more worthy...more righteous because they were the recipients of God's promises and His activity in their lives. I knew this...but I'd heard Jesus wasn't like that. Was He?

They seemed to move faster; now I was running after them.

"Oh Lord, Son of David, have mercy on me! My daughter suffers terribly!"

"Please stop, won't you?!"

"Oh God, I need You to heal my daughter!"

"Lord, have mercy on me!"

I guess I was somewhat of a bother. But I was not about to leave! All my hope was based on Jesus. I decided long ago that if Natalie was ever going to be released from her torment, Jesus was her only answer. We'd tried so many other useless, futile things. Only Jesus could give her relief. I don't know how I knew this; I just knew! In the depth of my spirit I knew He could make her well. When I waited by the road this morning, I was so sure. When I boldly waved for His attention, I was even excited. But now, as His disciples looked down their noses at me, and they all seemed to ignore me (even *Him*), I cringed with a new thought; what if He didn't want to?

I was thinking these things when one of the men shoved me and said, "Leave us alone! We're on vacation! We've left Galilee to find some rest! We didn't come to take care of anyone...we are not ministering now. Go away."

His words stung and sent my heart reeling into a desperate abyss. But just before my hopes were dashed, I gathered enough courage to bravely ignore his rebuke and press on toward Jesus. "Oh Lord! Have mercy on me!" I continued to plead, my voice was growing hoarse from so much yelling. I tugged on the sleeves of the women and tried to get them to look me in the eyes, "Please, tell Him to help me!"

"Stop for goodness sake! Don't pass me by!"

Finally they went to Him. "Send her away!" I heard one man say.

"No, don't, please don't! I need You, Lord!" My tears were choking my words, and they barely made sense anymore.

"She's bothering us!" Another one chimed in.

I just stood still and wept; even the women didn't say anything on my behalf.

Just when I was about to give up, Jesus turned to me and said, "I was sent only to the lost sheep of Israel."

"Uhh!" I caught my breath in my throat; He was talking to me. I finally had His undivided attention, and Jesus was talking directly to me! Immediately I knelt at His feet. I had said all I knew to say already—as I'd followed them all this way—so all I could choke out as my heart filled with the anguish of the past seven years was, "Lord, help me!"

"It's not right to take the children's bread and toss it to their dogs." He replied.

Strange, I thought. He didn't sound mad; He didn't even sound exasperated. He certainly didn't sound as if He were berating me. Instead, His words carried kindness that soothed my heart like a healing balm. I wondered for a moment at the contrast between what He said and the compassion in which He said it. I pondered His statement for a moment and made sure I'd heard Him correctly. As my ears took in the meaning of His words, I slowly lifted my head and glanced up at His face.

That's when my eyes met His.

Time stood still. The agony in my heart disappeared. I knew immediately, as I was lost in those warm portals of perfect love and sheer delight, that somehow I'd found the favor of God. He wasn't mad at all. There was no righteous indignation in Him, nor was there any disdain or pride. He didn't consider His gifts too precious to withhold them from the likes of me—even though I wasn't a daughter of Abraham.

In fact, in the moments we spent communicating with our eyes, I almost *saw* Him say, "Help me teach my disciples something here. Something you already know."

I smiled deep in my spirit, but immediately I dropped my head and in all humility responded, "Yes, Lord, but even the dogs eat the crumbs that fall from their masters' table."

Good answer! Jesus touched my head, lifted my face to look in His eyes again and said with a smile and a twinkle in those love filled eyes, "Woman, you have great faith. Your request is granted."

I knew Natalie was well at that very moment. I also knew in my heart what He didn't say out loud... "Thanks, for working with me on this."

From the Heart of the Woman Who Didn't Even Ask

Nathan was a joy to me. His father died when he was only 14, so it had been just the two of us for years. Even after enduring the desperate loss of Josiah, Nathan soon bounced back with his wit and humor. Although I didn't think I'd ever know true joy after my husband's death, Nathan helped me find my smile and even laughter again. We spent many evenings laughing over the simplest things as he told me stories of his day with all kinds of animation and sound effects.

Nathan never complained about having to work so hard at such a young age. Josiah left him with the weaving business in shambles. My husband was a sharp business man, and his records were meticulously kept; but his dedication to books caused him to fall short of the competition. People wanted to be coddled and made to feel good. Nathan came about this honestly. He asked me to help with the books so he could spend more time with our customers. I begged off because I'm no good at that sort of thing. The good Lord blessed me with the simple ability of being a wife and mother. Then the good Lord took away one of my jobs so I wanted to dedicate myself completely to the other. I didn't have any desire or ambition to be anything but Nathan's mother.

Nathan hired another young man to be his bookkeeper, and we enjoyed a peaceful, happy life. I looked forward to the day Nathan would marry and dreamt of the friendship I'd share with his wife. I also longed for children to fill our home with laughter. But a silent killer was to rob me of these dreams.

At first Nathan complained of headaches. I made strong herbal tea and provided him with warm cloths to place over his forehead. I urged him to stop working so hard, and he teased me about worrying far too much. I told him that was a mother's job!

Then the headaches grew worse. He came home from work in the middle of the day and went to his room. I hung dark fabric over his window to shut out all the light. I called the doctors, but they had no answers. I prayed, but Nathan grew worse. I hung dark fabric over all the windows in our house, thinking that I could swallow his pain in darkness. Nathan didn't laugh anymore. He stopped eating. His once robust body grew weak and thin. I told him I knew God would make him well, and he smiled weakly and squeezed my hand in gentle reply. One day I knelt by his bed and I started to cry. I thought he was beyond consciousness so I poured my desperate heart out as I looked at his pain stricken face.

Oh, Nathan. What will I do if you die? You are my only hope! I've only lived to be your father's wife and to be your mother? What else is there for me? You found my smile again after your father died, but if you leave me too—there will be no smile to be found. It will be gone for good.

He didn't squeeze my hand that day. He never squeezed it again.

It is our tradition to bury the body within 24 hours of death. I knew he was gone. His face was gray and his hands were cold as ice. Oh how I cried. Others cried too. All our friends came to mourn his death. So many people loved my sweet Nathan. He was taken out of this world far too soon! We were marching in the funeral procession. His body was exposed in the wooden casket in the front of our parade. It is our custom to smother the body with flowers and parade it in the streets as we allow the dead to be honored in this way.

I'm not sure how long we'd been walking when I heard these gentle words, "Don't cry."

They were more than words of sympathy; they were commanding words that seemed to say, "I have come and there's no longer any need for tears here."

I looked up with swollen eyes to see who would say such a thing and was nearly nose to nose with the most beautiful man I've ever seen. His touch was tender as He held His fingers on my elbow. His eyes were swimming with love and brimming with grief. Like flood water pouring over a dam, I saw tears spilling down His cheeks—each one glistening with all that I'd felt during Nathan's brief illness and death. And because we were both sobbing like babies, I wondered at His words... "Don't cry."

But amazingly, I stopped; almost immediately my tears ceased to flow. Maybe I was curious. Maybe I felt the surge of supernatural power flow from His fingertips into my soul. Maybe, when I looked into that sweet wonderful face I saw a man who had authority over death and life...and I believed He was about to give something precious to me.

At the exact moment that my tears stopped flowing, His stopped too. And as soon as He saw all was well with me, He walked over to Nathan's body, He touched the coffin and said, "Young man, I say to you, get up!"

Nathan opened his eyes...he stepped right out of that box, and immediately started talking! "Hey everybody, what are you doing here?" He smiled, we laughed and Jesus motioned for him to come to me. I nearly fainted in Nathan's embrace as he whispered into my ear, "Where's that smile, Mama? I want to hear you laugh!"

Jesus met me on the darkest day of my life. He embraced my pain and healed my heart's deepest wound. Jesus turned my mourning into dancing, all before I even took the time to ask.

Questions for Reflection

1. Why didn't the disciples become advocates for the Canaanite woman?

2. Do we determine who is and who is not worthy of God's touch today? Examine your life this past week. Who did you feel compassion toward? Who did you take time to encourage?

3. What do you do when God doesn't seem to be listening? Are you ever tempted to believe He doesn't care? What verses can you point to in order to combat this lie?

4. How does the picture of God's "tear collection" encourage you?

5. When did God's love and power amaze you?

6. What has God given to you before you ever even thought to ask?

Ask God To

• Be honored as you spend three minutes thanking Him for His goodness.
• Strengthen you to claim His Word when Satan comes at you with deception.
• Know that you accept the fact that He is good.

MY PRAYER FOR THIS WEEK

A VERSE TO MEMORIZE

For nothing is impossible with God.

—

Luke 1:37

Bonus Week

CHAPTER 7

I Am the Lord's Servant

WOMAN TOUCHED BY JESUS
Mary
Luke 1:26-55

INTRODUCTION
"May it be to me as You have said..."

What an incredible woman who was powerfully touched by Jesus. Mary didn't have a disease; she didn't have a desperate need or a sin filled past. She didn't even come seeking Him. Nevertheless, God came to her and chose her to carry His only begotten Son in her womb. God chose to allow her the experience of partnering with Him in a most intimate way. For nine months Jesus was part of Mary's body. What Mary ate, Jesus ate. Where Mary went, Jesus went. What Mary chose to listen to, Jesus heard. As His infant body grew and developed, Mary was the first one to feel the presence of His life moving within her. Take a minute to imagine that; the Son of God wiggling like tiny butterflies inside her body.

Tom and I were blessed with a trip to the Holy Land several years ago. I was overwhelmed at the reality of God's Word as we walked the streets Jesus walked. God gave me an "ah ha moment" even with the maps in the back of my Bible.

Ah ha! These maps represent real places!

I recognized that the stories I had heard all my life were based on historical fact. They were not make-believe stories written "a long time ago in a faraway place." They were eyewitness accounts recorded with accuracy and passed down through the ages.

But out of all the places we visited, the one that impacted me most was the cave where Mary and Joseph supposedly stayed the night Jesus was born. We were in Bethlehem. We waited in the incense-filled church for our turn to walk downstairs to a place in the basement area where tradition tells us Jesus was born.

Many of Israel's holy sites have been saved through the years by the construction of churches. Even in the midst of chaos in the Middle East, these sacred monuments provide some security to the holy sites. I determined early in my visit that the exact location of Jesus' miracles and milestones might not have been at the exact site the tour guide pointed us to. And I decided to overlook what the tourist industry did to the place (i.e. the plastic baby Jesus placed in a cradle on display behind a glass window in the cave), but even if the precise spot were unknown, you can be sure that what they are showing you is at least a good representation of what might have been some 2000 years ago.

Tom and I made our way down the damp stairs toward the basement, and the Holy Spirit brought the words of John 1:14 to my mind:

"The Word became flesh and dwelt among us, and we have seen His glory, the glory of the One and Only, who came from the Father, full of grace and truth."

We stood in an opening looking at stone walls and a dirt floor. The air was cool and damp. The tour guide pointed to a gold plate on the floor that marked the spot where Jesus was born. My imagination carried me back to that first Christmas Eve. I could almost hear the hustle and bustle of people as they crowded into the City of David to be counted in the census. I could imagine the innkeeper's concern as he looked at Joseph's desperate face, and I could almost see Mary double over with the next of a wave of contractions as Joseph rushed to spread blankets on the hard stable floor.

And then, I stared at that gold plate. And I wondered at the majesty and love of God that would allow His Son to be born into this world. I wondered at the glory of God that would allow His Son to come to us since we were unable to come to Him. I worshipped God in that cave because I knew that had the Word not become flesh and dwelt among us we could never have the opportunity to even begin to experience His glory. I thanked God for being full of grace and truth.

My prayer for you this week as we wrap up this study of women who were touched powerfully and personally by Jesus is that you will behold His glory, the glory of the One and Only who came from the Father, full of grace and truth.

DAY 1
GREETINGS TO YOU
WHO ARE HIGHLY FAVORED

Read Luke 1:26-28

Greetings to You Who Are Highly Favored

Imagine how you might have felt if you'd received such a greeting.
Circle the words that could describe your reaction:

fear   excitement   dread   confusion   wonder

Luke 1:29 says that, "Mary was *greatly troubled* at his words and *wondered* what kind of greeting this might be." And immediately, Gabriel responded to Mary's concern with a phrase angels seem to use often when they stand face to face with mankind: "Do not be afraid Mary, you have *found favor* with God."

> For nothing is impossible with God.
> Luke 1:37

How do you suppose Mary "found favor with God"? What did she do that caused God to "favor" her? If we could know this, perhaps we could "find favor with God" too!

Meet God in His Word

Turn to Psalm 37 and complete the statements. Read verses 3-6.
Trust in the Lord and do good;

Delight yourself in the Lord and

Commit your way to the Lord; trust in Him and He will do this:

Evil men will be cut off but those who hope in the Lord will (v. 9)

The meek will (v. 11)

The power of the wicked will be broken but the Lord (v. 17)

The days of the blameless are known to the Lord, and their inheritance will (v. 18)

If the Lord delights in a man's ways He (v. 23)

For the Lord loves the just and will not (v. 28)

Do you see some key words in these verses? What about *meek, righteous, just* and *faithful*. Take a moment to consider the meaning of these words:

Meek – humble, submissive, gentle, mild
Righteous – virtuous, moral, good, upright, honest, respectable, blameless
Just – truthful, fair, right, impartial, honest
Faithful – devoted, trustworthy, dependable, dedicated, committed, reliable

No doubt Mary, in her young life, had already placed her confidence in God. And because God considered her "highly favored," we can assume she was meek, righteous, just and faithful. Look again at those words. Think about the role Mary would play in God's tremendous redemption plan. Aren't all these characteristics absolutely necessary for whomever God would choose to be that intimately involved?

Face to Face with Jesus
Don't you want God to consider you "highly favored"? Don't you want to claim the promises we read in Psalm 37? If so, invite Jesus to touch you today. Go back to Psalm 37, read the following verses and answer these questions:

Verse 1: Do you fret because of evil men?

Verse 4: What is promised to you when you "delight yourself in the Lord"?

Verse 11: How do you suppose the "meek will inherit that land"?

Verses 23-24: Thank God for the promise in verse 24. Tell about a time God held you with His hand:

Do you need His strong hand today? Is there a place in your life where you want to experience His support? Print Psalm 37:39-40 in the space provided: Thank God for His deliverance.

MY PRAYER FOR TODAY

DAY 2
HIGHLY FAVORED BY GOD

Read Luke 1:26-38

God's Plan for My Life

If we're not careful we spend our lives looking for God's plan to feature us. We ask God, "What do you have for me today?" And what we really mean is, "What way do You plan to use *me* in your kingdom work for *my* good and *my* glory?"

> *For nothing is impossible with God.*
> Luke 1:37

Without realizing it, we often bump God out of the limelight and put ourselves in the "star" role of the drama called "My Life." Too often we offer God the supporting role in this drama, with His sole purpose being to make sure we come out looking good.

This is not what the Bible teaches!

Meet God in His Word

Mary found favor with God because her young life already exhibited firm reliance, faith, devotion and righteousness. Mary also found favor with God because of what she was about to experience.

Do not be afraid, Mary, you have found favor with God.

Go to Genesis 6:8. Who else found favor with God?

Which of these statements describe the meaning of the *favor of God?* Check the ones that apply:

- God has noticed your faithfulness and devotion.
- Your conscience is clear.
- God has a part for you to fulfill in His plan.
- God has created a plan that features you.

Consider Noah. Noah's role in the flood was the supporting role. He was not the star. Yes, he built the ark (no, he didn't design it!). Yes, he loaded all the animals on to the ark (no, he didn't close the door), and he survived the flood, thus preserving life. However it was God who caused the flood, God who kept the ark afloat, God who sustained life cooped up in the floating zoo and God who made the waters subside. In all actuality, Noah simply walked daily with God and did as he was told.

Face to Face with Jesus

God certainly has a plan for your life. But, it isn't about you. God's plan is about Him. He performs for His own glory, not for ours. God chooses to use those who "walk with Him" to take care of the details of His plan in the world today. Would you be willing to lay aside your list of expectations and desires? Would you be willing to step aside—out of the spotlight—and embrace the role of supporting actress? Would you dedicate your life to making Jesus look good to others? If so, tell God today.

MY PRAYER FOR TODAY

DAY 3
HOW CAN THIS BE?

Read Luke 1:31-33

Prophecies Fulfilled

When Mary asked Gabriel, "How can this be?" Gabriel referenced prophecies concerning the promised Messiah.

Read Isaiah 7:14. Which prophecy did God fulfill through Mary?

Read 2 Samuel 7:16. Which prophecy did Gabriel make reference to?

Other prophecies Gabriel connected his revelation to are found in Psalm 89:3-4; Isaiah 9:7; Jeremiah 33:17; Daniel 2:44, 7:14, 27; and Micah 4:7. By making reference to all these prophecies, Gabriel was assuring Mary that Jesus was the Messiah, sent by God to fulfill all His promises to His people.

> *For nothing is impossible with God.*
> Luke 1:37

Meet God in His Word

When Mary responded to Gabriel's declaration, she was not concerned about God's ability to bring the promised Messiah. What concerned her was *how* God would choose that the Messiah be conceived in her since she was still a virgin. Mary felt unqualified for such a task.

Read Luke 1:35 carefully. Print the verse in the space provided.

193

Let's stop right here. When God chooses to find you highly favored, when He chooses to use you to impact His kingdom work, He will accomplish His work through you by the strength and power of His Holy Spirit. Too often we come prepared to put our gifts, talents and abilities to work *for* Him. Too often we shrink back from participating in the adventure of kingdom service, for in comparison to others, our gifts, talents and abilities seem terribly inadequate!

"How can this be...since I am a virgin?"

But **God** performs His work in the strength and power of His Holy Spirit! So, the Holy One receives the glory. God performs the impossible in and through us. The very thing Mary thought might *disqualify* her for the assignment, actually *qualified* her for God's assignment!

Read I Corinthians 1:27-29.

God chose the _____ things of the world to shame the

_____.

God chose the _____ things of the world to shame the

_____.

He chose the _____ things of this world and the

_____ things–and the things that are _____

to nullify the things that _____, so that...

No one may boast before Him!

Remember Saint Francis of Assisi? When God wishes to confound the wise, He chooses the unwise. When He wishes to amaze the learned, He chooses the uneducated. When God wants to reveal Himself to the world, He chooses to work in and through men and women who recognize "He is God and we are not."

Face to Face with Jesus

Read Luke 1:36-37. God performs the impossible in and through us. Will you echo Mary's response to God? Will you humbly respond to God's call to you? Can you join Mary and say:

"I am the Lord's servant, may it be done to me as you have said."

Tell God you want Him to be glorified in your life. Remember, when God chooses to work powerfully through you... "the Holy Spirit will come upon you and the power of the Most High will overshadow you."

Praise His Holy Name!

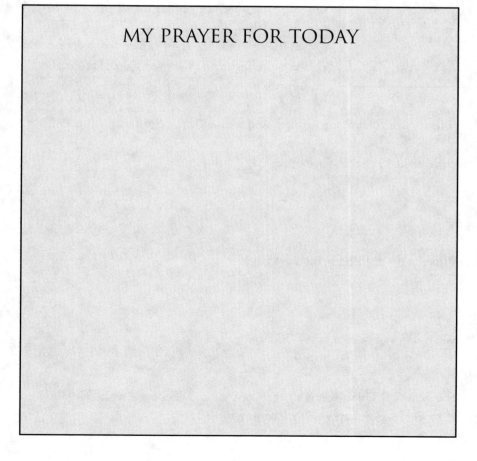

MY PRAYER FOR TODAY

DAY 4
BLESSED IS SHE WHO HAS BELIEVED

Read Luke 1:39-45

"Blessed Is She Who Has Believed!"

Wouldn't you like that said of you? "Blessed is she who has believed!"

What a wonderful God we serve. When He chooses to use us, He works all around us to take care of us. Gabriel told Mary that God was already doing the impossible in Elizabeth's life. A woman infertile for years, and now past her child-bearing years, was pregnant! This pregnancy gave Mary an example of God's ability to do the impossible. This pregnancy also gave Mary a safe place to go during her own crisis pregnancy. Pregnant, unwed teens were not only frowned upon in Mary's day; legally they could be stoned.

> *For nothing is impossible with God.*
> Luke 1:37

Rather than being the recipient of rejection and righteous indignation, Mary was greeted at Elizabeth's house with joy!

"Blessed are you among women, and blessed is the child you will bear."

Print verse 45 in the space provided:

What credit did Elizabeth give Mary?

What did Mary do to bring God's glory?

She believed! This gives us a key to how we can cooperate with God and join Him in His kingdom work: we choose to BELIEVE!

196

Meet God in His Word

Look up the following verses. They present examples of women who chose to believe God. Beside each name, tell what she did as a result of her choice to believe.

Shiprah and Puah (Exodus 1:20-22)

Ruth (Ruth 4:13-16)

Rahab (Joshua 6:17, 22-23, 25)

In your own words describe how God responded to their choice to believe:

Shiprah and Puah (Exodus 1:20-22)

Ruth (Ruth 4:13-16)

Rahab (Joshua 6:17, 22-23, 25)

Face to Face with Jesus

God does not require you to have a master's degree from a seminary. (Nor does He ignore the fact that you might have one!) God does not require you to have a voice that sounds like angels (though He gifts some of you with one!). God does not require the ability to speak eloquently. He doesn't require management skills, accounting skills, ten years' experience, and leadership traits. In order to be used powerfully in God's kingdom work, He merely requires you to **BELIEVE!**

When is the last time you took God at His Word?

Print Luke 1:37.

Step out and BELIEVE God's Word by printing something in this space that is impossible—something you'd like for Him to do that would bring glory to Him.

Can Elizabeth's blessing be said of you? "Blessed is she who believed that what the Lord has said to her will be accomplished."

MY PRAYER FOR TODAY

DAY 5
MARY'S SONG...MARY'S TEARS

Read Luke 1:46-55

Mary's Song

We catch a glimpse of the depth of Mary's spirit when we read her song. She sang it at Elizabeth's house. Notice that she was in the presence of other believers who were also experiencing God's supernatural involvement in their own lives.

God means for us to function on earth as a Body of Believers...not as soloists but as a choir. One person may be featured at one time, and another one featured at another time. But remember that the STAR of your life performance is God, not you. The Christian journey is not about us but about Christ.

> *For nothing is impossible with God.*
> Luke 1:37

Mary sang her song freely in the comforting fellowship of other believers. That is where we sing best. Make sure you allow yourself to love and be loved by a family of faith. You will fall far short of God's best for your life if you choose to live apart from strong fellowship with other believers.

Note all the ways Mary expressed her spirit:

Verse 46: My soul *glorifies* the Lord.

Verse 47: My spirit *rejoices in* God my savior.

Verse 48: From now on all generations will call me *blessed*.

Verse 49: For the Mighty One has done *great things* for me.

Meet God in His Word

Compare Mary's song to that of Hannah in I Samuel 2:1-10. Fill in the Blanks that describe how Hannah felt when she prayed:

My heart _____ in the Lord; in the Lord my horn is lifted _____. My mouth _____ over my enemies, for I _____ in your deliverance.

What common threads do you find in these verses?

I Samuel 2:1 and Luke 1:46-47

I Samuel 2:4 and Luke 1:51

I Samuel 2:5 and Luke 1:53

I Samuel 2:6-8 and Luke 1:52

I Samuel 2:9-10 and Luke 1:50, 54-55

Consider what God's answer to Hannah's prayer for a son cost her. Hannah's prayer was written right after she took young Samuel to the temple and left him there to live with Eli. Hannah would no longer hear Samuel say, "Kiss and hug!" when she put him to bed at night; she'd never give in to "Please read me just one more page!" Nor would she ever again reach for an apple to offer him when he begged, "I'm hungry; can I have a snack?" Hannah took the miracle answer to her heart cry and gave him back to God by sending him to live with an old priest who'd already failed miserably at rearing his own sons. How do you think Hannah felt when she left Samuel with Eli?

How would you have felt?

Read the following verses and consider what God's favor cost Mary. John 19:25-27 and Mark 15.

Face to Face with Jesus:
Mary and Hannah both found favor with God. Their participation in God's kingdom activity brought them great joy at the expense of deep hurt. Hannah's Samuel anointed David king—the king to whom God promised to continue a royal lineage that would last forever. Mary's baby boy became the Savior of the world, thus establishing David's throne just as God had promised.

Choosing to invest your life in God's kingdom work is not something you do lightly or flippantly. Choosing to give up control of your today and your tomorrow is a solemn decision based on your choice to believe that God loves you and will ultimately fulfill all His promises toward you. When God finds favor with you, you may still experience deep sorrow and pain; but you will also discover strength, peace, and joy to sustain you as you fix your eyes not on what is seen but on what is unseen.

"For what is seen is temporary, but what is unseen is eternal."
2 Corinthians 4:18

If you would like to link your heart with the heart of God, tell Him so right now. Say, "Lord, I believe that nothing is impossible with You. I trust you with my whole heart; therefore, I too join Mary again and declare, "I am the Lord's servant, may it be done to me as you have said."

If you prayed this prayer, you just made a commitment to God, not a "bargain."

MY PRAYER FOR TODAY

From the Heart of Mary
(A story based on several Scripture passages)

She felt something warm splash on her neck then trickle down her back, but the pain in her heart far outweighed any other sensation. The ground was rough and full of rocks that cut into her shins as she desperately tried to bow herself low and absorb the reality of this day. She rhythmically bumped her forehead against the splinter-filled, rugged wood in an effort to give some sort of desperate expression to her indescribable pain.

"Aaaaauuuu!" Oh how she longed to cry out. But there were no sounds deep enough to give voice to her sorrow. So instead of opening her mouth, she drug her now bleeding knees even closer to where the soldiers had thumped that post into the ground. She wrapped her gentle arms around that Roman symbol of authority and shame and didn't even notice when the splinters dug into her soft hands.

It was as close to her dying son as she could get.

Mary, did you know? That little boy would one day be a king.

"No, I didn't know. I didn't know I'd be here today."

Mary was unaware of the others around her. Their mocking didn't have any effect on her. She was all alone at the cross that day. And though her body knelt where His blood spilled, Mary was far, far away. It was late in the morning and she was only 15.

"Greetings to you who are highly favored! The Lord is with you!"

What did He mean by that? Mary remembered the day that changed everything. She remembered the innocent wonder. She smiled again at Gabriel's calm assurance that the power of the Most High God would overshadow her. Mary remembered.

"Oh God, Most High...I desperately need the power of your Holy Spirit to overshadow me this instant!"

Mary heard a noise...

"Oh Jesus, don't try to talk; it won't be long now and you'll be back where you belong!

"Oh Jesus..." She looked up at His face. He bent His head so that His swollen bloodshot eyes were looking into her own, and in a gurgling whisper He said, "Dear woman, here is your Son."

As He forced the words out of His collapsing chest, He glanced over toward John. "What? Where? You are my Son, dear Jesus...bleeding and dying Oh God, I need You now!" He was motioning to His dearly loved friend and disciple, John. John's own face filled with torment. But he caught the meaning of his Master's words, and immediately John came to Mary. He nodded understanding and wrapped his arms around her trembling shoulders. When John did this, Jesus nodded slowly and almost whispered again in a guttural noise, "Here is your mother." He said to John.

"Thank You, Lord. Even as You die, You're meeting my every need." Mary wondered at how God could be so attentive. With the strength of John's shared grief, once again Mary was far away in her thoughts. She remembered how full of joy and wonder she was when she responded to Gabriel, "I am the Lord's servant, may it be to me as you have said."

How could she have possibly known that commitment would cost her so? Even after she'd said them, Mary remembered how the reality of Gabriel's words began to soak in, and how she was afraid to tell her mother and father about her pregnancy. Would they understand? What would she do? Mary remembered how Mama suggested she go visit Elizabeth and see for herself this miracle pregnancy Gabriel told her about. If Elizabeth were pregnant, then what Gabriel said had to be true. The family knew of Elizabeth's barrenness and no woman (save Sarah) conceived and gave birth at such an age!

How could she ever forget Elizabeth's greeting? "Blessed are you among women!"

Mary remembered how blessed she felt!

"My soul glorifies the Lord and my spirit rejoices in God my Savior!!"

And did she ever rejoice! It was at Elizabeth's home that the full impact of God's choosing her began to envelop her with wonder. God was bringing the promised Messiah, and He was bringing Him as a baby—her baby. Mary smiled at the memory of those gentle days...the days before life became so complicated. Neither she nor Elizabeth had any clue what their partnership with God would demand of them.

"Oh God, thank You for Elizabeth's faith. What grace she demonstrated when You took John from her!"

Another splash of crimson liquid on her neck, and the warmth of the trickle abruptly interrupted her moment of reflection as it ran down her back.

"Oh God, how can this be?" Mary wondered. She realized His very life was dripping away.

Mary remembered the night He was born. The pregnancy had been amazing. After her sickness went away, she lay awake at night talking to Him as He moved in her womb. She wondered how God could do something so amazing and choose her to be part of it. She thanked God again and again for trusting her with such a task. Mary remembered how gentle Joseph was. A pang of grief stabbed her already heavy heart as she recalled his death. Joseph was always the gentle, good provider, lover and friend. They were partners together in this! Mary couldn't have survived Jesus' birth without him. She smiled as she remembered how he'd taken care of all the details while she suffered the pains of labor. She remembered how Joseph shook with wonder when he presented her with the precious bundle of holiness. She remembered how the two of them counted his fingers and toes in those first few hours when they were all alone with him in that stable. Thank You, Lord, for Joseph.

Mary remembered how He'd nursed at her very own breast. She peeled her arms from the rugged cross and pressed them to her breast while John shifted to make room for her to move. Sweet, gentle John—even in his own grief he was looking out for her needs.

"Jesus...I nursed You!"

"Oh God."

Mary looked up at His feet. He was shifting them in search for some sort of relief from the suffocating pressure filling His lungs with fluid as He hung on that cross. Those feet, those precious feet. Mary remembered cuddling his feet. He loved to have His toes tickled. She remembered when He took His first step and how He laughed when He toddled all the way from her arms to the arms of Joseph stretched out to hold Him.

Oh, the places those feet had been. She stretched her hand up the cross in an attempt to press her fingertips to His toes, but they hung just out of her reach. Two other times she hadn't been able to reach Him. The time He gave them such a fright when He stayed behind at the temple, talking with the Pharisees. She remembered how frantic she was when she thought they'd lost Him. Throughout His young life Mary felt protective. She would never forget how she and Joseph wrapped Him up in blankets and shushed Him as they fled to Egypt in the middle of the night when He was only a toddler. She realized then that He would have enemies who would pursue Him possibly throughout His life. She and Joseph felt responsible for His well-being. She remembered the fears that pressed against her heart when she looked and looked but couldn't find Him anywhere among family and friends that day.

Then she remembered how amazed she was when she stood at the edge of the circle of religious leaders who were captivated by Him as He taught the teachers in the temple. And she wondered how a 12-year-old boy could be so wise.

Mary also remembered the other time she couldn't reach Him. Once again she felt the twinge of hurt when she'd heard Him say, "Behold my mother and my brothers! For whoever does the will of my Father in heaven is my brother and sister and mother."

She'd known from the beginning that He was not hers. But hers was a unique role. She fed and clothed Him, rocked and bathed Him. She spent hours talking and listening to Him. She knew He was God's Son and that she was God's partner in bringing Him here.

The sky grew unusually dark. Mary didn't notice the people that fell in fear all around her. She didn't hear the Roman soldiers whisper. She didn't sense any of the oppression others seemed to sense. Mary turned her eyes toward the heavens and listened for God to speak to her once again.

Mary remembered His laughter. She remembered His tears. She remembered how He loved without fear and how He always responded to people with kindness and compassion. She saw snapshots of Him turning water into wine. She could almost hear the festivities of the wedding that day. She saw Him baptized and thought for a moment she caught the flutter of dove's wings flapping in the wind. Mary heard the Pharisees accusations as they confronted Him on so many occasions. She observed the weariness she saw in His eyes when the crowds followed Him even as He sought to go away and rest. She saw Him looking her way as He told the disciples another parable.

For three hours Mary knelt at the foot of the cross and heard His voice—she saw His face. She never once saw Him grimace or heard Him complain.

Gabriel's words echoed in her ears...

"He will reign over the house of Jacob forever; his kingdom will never end."

"How can this be? This cross is definitely an end to Jesus' life. Did something go wrong?" Mary felt another splash of blood as Jesus hung silently suspended between earth and heaven just above her head. "What did You mean, Lord? The shepherds said the angels sang! 'Glory to God in the highest and peace on earth...' Were we too corrupt to embrace Your peace?"

Mary wondered, and the sky grew darker.

Then, a cloud began to lift in Mary's heart. In her mind, she heard Jesus speak as she pondered the things He taught:

"If anyone would come after Me, he must deny himself and take up his cross daily and follow Me."

What did this cross have to do with His kingdom?

"For God so loved the world that He gave His one and only Son that whoever believes in Him shall not perish but have eternal life. For God did not send His Son into the world to condemn the world but to save the world through Him."

"Eternal life...He taught about life in heaven with His Father. A different life, a life beyond the grave! He came that we might have life...abundant life He called it." Mary wondered at these words, "I am the resurrection and the life."

He healed the sick, made the lame walk again. He gave sight to the blind and opened deaf ears. He brought people back from the dead! "If His death was not part of God's plan, He wouldn't be dying. He certainly had power over life and death! Jesus chose to hang on that cross. It was the Father's plan!"

Mary slowly rose to stand. She'd been bent down so long that her legs shook as she unfolded them and stepped back from the foot of the cross. She looked up at the dying body of her beloved Jesus and again she heard these words: "My heart is troubled and what shall I say, 'Father, save me from this hour?' No, it was for this very reason I came to this hour. Father glorify Your name!"

"This is why He came! This is why God brought Him here! Behold the lamb of God, who takes away the sins of the world! He is bearing the weight of our guilt and shame. He is dying so we can live! He is taking on the sins of the world!"

Understanding welled up in Mary's soul. She stumbled and fell again to her knees, "He's taking on my sin too."

Mary thought about her life before Gabriel greeted her that day, and of how even in her innocent youth she too felt the desperate need for a Savior. Mary longed for a bridge between her own heart and the heart of God.

Mary remembered how she'd fallen short plenty of times from the holiness of God as a child and as an adult. She realized that the way to the Father was through His Son.

"For God so loved the world that He gave His only begotten Son, Jesus to die for me! God gave Jesus through me and for me!" Mary thanked God for sending Jesus to make the way for her and so many others to come to Him.

A tiny smile formed on her lips when Mary's wonder was interrupted by Jesus' loud shout. Unlike the other words He'd spoken from the cross, this time His voice was loud and vibrant with the same authority that had astounded the rulers and set the captives free.

"It is finished!"

And then He breathed His last. Silence. There was complete...penetrating silence.

Mary looked around her. For the first time, she noticed the people who were at the cross with her. So many people were lost and confused. The hope they had seemed to hang on that cross. Even the Pharisees looked shaken and afraid. They didn't understand what had just happened. Everyone's eyes reflected pain and desperation. They felt like she did when she first knelt there.

Mary was not sure what to do next, but she sensed some sort of supernatural peace flooding her broken heart. Mary rubbed her hand behind her neck and drew her palms close to her face so that she could examine His blood she wiped from there. In a silent prayer of deep sorrow mingled with incredible gratitude and undeniable peace, she remembered how this had all begun. Not this morning...not last night...not even when Judas chose to sell Him out. Mary remembered the day Gabriel greeted her with his unusual salutation. She remembered her total trust and dependence on God. And with the memory of that flooding her mind and heart, she prayed again...

"I am still Your servant, Lord.
Be it done to me as You have said."

Questions for Reflection

1. What characteristics might you embrace in order to be a woman who finds "favor with God"?

2. What is the difference between searching for *God's plan for my life* and discovering *God's plan*?

3. How did God take care of Mary through her pregnancy?

4. What must we do in order to cooperate with God and join Him in His kingdom work?

5. Based on the women you read about this week, how does God respond to our choosing to believe?

6. What does it mean: "God means for us to function on earth as a body of believers...not as soloists, but as a choir"?

7. What will it mean to you if you join Mary and pray, "I am the Lord's servant, may it be done to me as you have said"?

Ask God To

- Link your heart intimately, powerfully with His. Tell Him you trust Him with your whole heart.
- Create in you a clean heart as you seek to find favor with Him.
- Use you anyway He deems best. Pray, "I am the Lord's servant, may it be done to me as You have said."

MY PRAYER FOR THIS WEEK

From the Heart of Leighann

Ever since Jesus walked on earth, He's continued to touch women and redeem their lives. I've been touched by Jesus, and I hope that you have too. Here's my story.

My mother and father were Christians, faithful in church. Through the cradle roll at First Baptist Church, Union, South Carolina, I was enrolled in Sunday School before I ever took my first breath. I have a tiny little Bible the church gave me at my birth that commemorates this introduction to my spiritual development.

By the time I was nine years old, I knew Jesus died on the cross for me so that I could live with Him in heaven someday. I knew that in order to go to heaven when I die I had to invite Jesus into my heart and walk the aisle in my very large church to tell everyone there that I wanted to be baptized. I had no problem with inviting Jesus into my heart, but I just couldn't walk that aisle! The sanctuary was big, and few people ever "walked the aisle." When they did, they were put on the spot in front of everyone. The pastor pulled them close to his side and said, "Aren't we glad Henrietta has asked Jesus into her heart to be her Savior and to save her from all her sins?"

He always seemed gladder than anyone else, but gradually you'd hear a solemn "amen." And everyone would raise their hands to show their support in Henrietta's desire to "unite with the church in Christian fellowship."

I didn't want to have to be pulled close to the pastor in front of all those people and admit to them that I had sin in my life! I certainly didn't want someone to "amen" my sin, and the thought of "uniting with them in Christian fellowship" was confusing to me!

But, the Holy Spirit reminded me each Sunday during the invitation portion of our morning services that I needed to ask Jesus into my heart. He pestered me so much that I eventually had to squeeze the pew in front of me to hold my feet still and keep them from stepping toward the dreaded aisle! This was most difficult when we sang, "All to Jesus I surrender, all to Him I freely give. I will ever love and trust Him, in His presence daily live. I surrender all (not today), I surrender all (maybe next week), all to Jesus I surrender, I surrender all (whew—made it!).

On the way home from church one Sunday I asked my father, "Do you have to be baptized in order to go to heaven?" He gave me the great theological answer, "Certainly not! Baptism doesn't save you. To be saved you just have to ask Jesus into your heart."

I still remember the sense of relief I felt by his answer. I told God, "OK, this is what we'll do. I'll wait until I'm on my bed and am very old and I will ask You into my heart just in time to meet You in heaven. That way I'll never have to walk that aisle, be set apart as a sinner and be welcomed into the unity of Christian fellowship!"

But, that was not the answer the Holy Spirit was looking for. He never stopped pestering me, and I had to continue clinging to the pew during each week's invitation portion of the service. The summer after my sixth grade year in school, I attended GA camp (Girls in Action is a missions organization). On the first night of camp, my very excited, recently saved college-aged counselor asked each of us to introduce ourselves and tell when we'd been baptized. I froze in my bed. What did she mean putting us on the spot like that? I only knew one person in the cabin and was certain I was the only girl there who had yet to get up enough nerve to be baptized. It really wasn't any of her business. The sanctuary at her home church was most likely not as big and scary as mine. Fear started creeping into my belly. Why didn't the Holy Spirit leave me alone?

When it was my turn to share, I took my cue from another girl, Jan Bradshaw from Warm Springs (Wahm Sprangs), Georgia. She simply introduced herself, told where she went to church and left out the part about baptism. I did the same: "I'm Leighann Keesee, I'm from Powder Springs, Georgia and I attend FBC, Marietta."

My counselor didn't say a word. (I have a sneaking suspicion that she did talk to God about me all that week.) But she didn't have to talk to me because the Holy Spirit continued speaking to me loud and clear. Every day we sang this song:

"Life was filled with guns and wars and everyone got trampled on the floor. I wish we'd all been ready!... Two men walking up a hill, one was gone and one was standing still, I wish we'd all been ready!"

Suddenly the thought struck me; what if Jesus came and I never made it to that deathbed—what then? What if I died before I was ready; what then?

I tried to enjoy the week. We were celebrating Christmas in July. We had secret angels and left one another little gifts in socks we hung on the foot of our beds. I made bracelets and treasure boxes. We cooked over campfires and shared kitchen clean-up duty. On the last night of camp, the missionary who was spending the week with us sang, "O Holy Night." While he was singing, the Holy Spirit started again: "Leighann, did you know that if you'd been the only person in the entire world who'd ever done anything wrong, God would have still sent Jesus to be born that holy night? Did you know that if you'd been the only one who needed Him to provide a way for you to live with Him forever, He'd still let that baby boy grow up to be a man and die on the cross for you? Leighann, did you know God loves you this much? Did you know God loves you regardless of your sin? Did you know God wants to be with you in a personal, powerful way? Do you know He wants you to let Him in right now? Leighann, I stand at the door of your heart, and I'm knocking. Will you let Me come in?"

That was enough...finally I cried out in my heart, "Lord Jesus, I know that I'm a sinner! I've done so many things that are not right, including not asking You into my life years ago! Please come into my heart, forgive me of my sin and be my Savior! I want You to be my best friend. I want to give You my life! Amen."

Immediately joy flooded my heart. I could hardly sit still. Tears streamed down my face. I knew, I *knew* the Holy Spirit was no longer pestering me from the outside; He'd come in. He was setting up residence in my life. I felt as if my heart would burst from the warmth and peace that swelled in it. This was what my heart was created to feel.

As soon as we returned to our cabins, I told my counselor I'd asked Jesus to be my Savior. She cried, all my new friends cried...and Jan shared with us that she'd invited Jesus into her heart too. All of us huddled together in a tight little circle crying, praying and celebrating our personal encounters with God through the blood sacrifice of His Son, Jesus.

For many years prior to my salvation experience I understood God loved His world. From the time I participated in preschool Vacation Bible School, I knew I John 4:16: "God is love." My VBS and Sunday School teachers taught us of God's love for the world when we made muslin banners of the hymn, "This is my Father's world." We memorized John 3:16: "For God so loved THE WORLD, that He gave..." God's love embraces the world. His heart wraps around our globe.

But knowing (and even accepting) that God loves His world is not enough. There comes a time in each person's life when she has to decide whether to accept or reject God's gracious invitation to know Him personally. Let me see if I can describe this difference between having an understanding of God—and entering into a personal relationship with Him—by using an illustration from my marriage:

When we were in seminary at Southwestern Baptist Theological Seminary in Ft. Worth, Texas, my roommate Georgia had her eye on Tom McCoy. While driving down McCart Avenue, she pointed Tom out to me at a red light. He drove a chocolate brown Audi 5000 with tinted windows. As I strained for a glimpse of his face, I caught it, and, now, I knew Tom. Not long after that, Georgia introduced me to what she considered this "hunk of a man." On that particular Sunday night, I entertained Tom (and his roommate Bert) while Georgia took a long distance phone call from one of her brothers. (The Lord works in mysterious ways.) Now, I knew Tom and Tom knew me.

After Tom and Bert left, Georgia and I prayed they'd invite us out on a double date. (This is what all good seminary girls do, of course!) While she voiced the prayer out loud, I exercised my wonderful privilege of silent prayer. "Lord," Georgia prayed in her most reverent voice, "let Tom ask me out, and Bert ask Leighann out on a double date. That would be so fun!"

To which I silently added, "Lord, really if it's not too much trouble, I'd actually enjoy getting to know Tom better than Bert." Apparently God honored my silent privilege. Several dates, discussions, intimate encounters, wedding, honeymoon, term papers, graduation, door knocking, business meetings, infertility tests, jobs, vacations, shocks, deaths, births, church buildings, successes and years later...after 21+ years of marriage, today I can tell you I *know* Tom McCoy.

When I asked Jesus to be my Savior on a Thursday night at camp in the north Georgia mountains, I began to know God in much the same way I began to know Tom when I said, "I do" on January 3, 1987. At the moment of my conversion, I understood that the God who so loved the world also loved me. But little did I know where that journey would take me. As I grow more intimately acquainted with Jesus, I embrace the things His heart embraces. My prayer today is that my heart will beat with the passion of His heart.

The goal of our journey on earth is to embrace and be embraced by the heart of God. As we grow in our intimacy with God, we'll grow in our effectiveness in His kingdom work. God's love is perfect, and His task is what you were crafted to complete. Your contentment, joy and fulfillment in this life will be in direct proportion to the degree to which you allow your heart to embrace the heart of God. May He continue to amaze you with His love as you follow Him on your life's great adventure.

Other Women Touched by Jesus

Peter's mother-in-law	Matthew 8:14-17, Luke 4:38-39
The mother of James and John	Matthew 20:20-28
Many women at the cross	Matthew 27:55-56, Mark 15:42-47, Luke 23:55-56, John 19:25-27
Women at the Resurrection	Matthew 28:1-10, Mark 16:1-11, Luke 24:1-11, John 20:10-18
Widow with an offering	Mark 12:41-44, Luke 21:1-4
Elizabeth	Luke 1:39-45, 57-80
Anna the prophetess	Luke 2:36-38
A crippled woman	Luke 13:10-13

Women Touched by God
(IN THE OLD TESTAMENT)

Eve	Genesis 2-4
Sarah	Genesis 12, 15-18:15, 20-23
Rebekah	Genesis 24-25, 27
Rachel	Genesis 29-35
Leah	Genesis 29-35
Tamar	Genesis 38
Moses' mother	Genesis 2
Miriam	Genesis 2, 15; Numbers 12
Pharoah's daughter	Genesis 2
Daughters of Zelophehad	Numbers 27:1-11
Rahab	Joshua 2, 6
Deborah	Judges 4-5
Delilah	Judges 16
Naomi and Ruth	Ruth
Hannah	I Samuel 1-2
Michal	I Samuel 18:18-30, 19, 25:44; II Samuel 3:6-16, 6:16-23
Abigail	I Samuel 25, 27, 30, II Samuel 2:1-4, 3:3
Bathsheba	II Samuel 11-12; I Kings 1:28-53
Tamar	II Samuel 13
Queen of Sheba	I Kings 10
Widow at Zarepath	I Kings 17
Widow with oil	II Kings 4
Shunammite woman	II Kings 4, 8
Naaman's servant girl	II Kings 5
Esther	Esther
Job's wife	Job
Two adulterous sisters	Ezekiel 23
Ezekiel's wife	Ezekiel 24
Gomer	Hosea

NOTES AND PRAYERS FROM YOUR HEART

BOOKS AND RESOURCES AVAILABLE FROM PRAY ALL THE WAY MINISTRIES:

Pray All the Way: From Fear to Faith
A Prayer Journey in the Shadow of Giants

A 30-day devotional guide that challenges you to become a giant slayer. As you camp out with David in I Samuel 17, you will discover many similarities between the Israelite army and today's church. You will also discover how your personal relationship with God can transform your fear to faith (just as David's did for him).

Pray All the Way: From Glory unto Glory

A 30-day devotional guide. Does God enjoy seeing His church limp along in a fallen world? What must we do in order to receive all that God has to give? What will you do to prepare your heart and your mind to engage in divine partnership so that God's glory will be revealed in and through your life? These are the questions this book will answer.

Oh God, Please! The Heart Cry of a Burdened Soul

A 10-week prayer study that explores the prayer lives of several men and women in the Bible who discovered the adventure of intimate partnership with God. The study takes you from David's "Oh God, Please!" prayer in Psalm 143 to Paul's declaration of victory in Romans 11:33-36. Along the way you will examine your own concept of God's power and love. Step by step Leighann leads you to apply the bold promises in God's Word that deal with the reality of God's desire to work His power and love in and through your life. The 11 teaching sessions on DVD and audio CD are sold separately. DVD is essential for group study.

Pray Right!

James 5:16 says, "The prayer of a righteous man is powerful and effective." By participating in this three-part (four weeks each) study, you will discover the truth of James' words by discovering how righteousness releases power in your prayer life. You will then practice praying:
- From a "right" posture
- From a "right" perspective
- For "right" purposes

This study has 10 DVD teaching sessions and audio CDs sold separately. DVD is essential for group study.

About the Author

Leighann McCoy serves on staff at Thompson Station Church in Thompson Station, Tennessee as prayer and women's minister. Leighann is the wife of Tom (senior pastor at Thompson Station Church) and the mother of daughters Mikel and Kaleigh and son TJ.

She leads women's retreats and prayer conferences throughout the country and is a frequent contributor to her denomination's ministry as a conference leader and writer.

Leighann received her bachelor's degree from Samford University and her master's degree from Southwestern Baptist Theological Seminary.

For more information regarding Leighann's ministry, or to order resources, you may contact her at www.prayalltheway.com